Acclaim for Robert D. Kaplan's

WARRIOR POLITICS

"Timely as well as thoughtful. . . . Kaplan's warnings about Osama bin Laden, bioterrorism, and a volatile future . . . were prescient when they were written, well before September 11, 2001."
—*The National Interest*

"An important book that cautions against the well-intentioned liberal idea that we should export the political ideas that have worked in this country to areas of the world that lack our history, literacy, economic success, and egalitarian culture." —*Houston Chronicle*

"A provocative book. Tough measures and tragic choices will be necessary to win the war on terror, and revisiting Kaplan's preferred political thinkers will hardly lead us astray." —*National Review*

"Kaplan skillfully captures the relevance of classical political theory for today's leaders, whether they manage crises in the boardroom or the Oval Office." —William S. Cohen, former secretary of defense

"The reason I have come to admire Bob Kaplan's little book . . . is its refusal to apologize for its analogies. This is so refreshing. . . . What Kaplan is saying—and what Hobbes and Machiavelli and some of the Founders said—was that such realism is in fact *more* moral than idealism. Idealism in state craft is based on an abdication of responsibility—to govern the world as it is." —Andrew Sullivan

Robert D. Kaplan

WARRIOR POLITICS

Robert D. Kaplan is a correspondent for *The Atlantic Monthly* and the bestselling author of eight previous books on foreign affairs and travel, including *Balkan Ghosts, The Ends of the Earth, The Coming Anarchy,* and *Eastward to Tartary.* He lives with his wife and son in western Massachusetts.

ALSO BY ROBERT D. KAPLAN

Eastward to Tartary:
Travels in the Balkans, the Middle East, and the Caucasus

The Coming Anarchy: Shattering the Dreams of the Post Cold War

An Empire Wilderness: Travels into America's Future

The Ends of the Earth:
From Togo to Turkmenistan, from Iran to Cambodia,
a Journey to the Frontiers of Anarchy

The Arabists: The Romance of an American Elite

Balkan Ghosts: A Journey Through History

Soldiers of God:
With Islamic Warriors in Afghanistan and Pakistan

Surrender or Starve: The Wars Behind the Famine

WARRIOR POLITICS

The side that knows when to fight and when not will take the victory. There are roadways not to be traveled, armies not to be attacked, walled cities not to be assaulted.

SUN-TZU

Anyone wishing to see what is to be must consider what has been: all the things of this world in every era have their counterparts in ancient times.

MACHIAVELLI

WARRIOR POLITICS

WHY LEADERSHIP

DEMANDS

A PAGAN ETHOS

ROBERT D. KAPLAN

Vintage Books

A Division of Random House, Inc.

New York

FIRST VINTAGE BOOKS EDITION, JANUARY 2003

The Library of Congress has cataloged the Random House edition as follows:
Kaplan, Robert D.
Warrior politics : why leadership demands a Pagan ethos /
Robert D. Kaplan.—1st ed.
p. cm.
Includes bibliographical references and index.
ISBN 0-375-50563-6 (alk. Paper)
1. International relations—Psychological aspects.
2. International relations—Political aspects. 3. Leadership.
4. Political ethics. I. Title
JZ1253 .K37 2002
320'.01'9—dc21
2001031862

Vintage ISBN: 978-0-375-72627-9

Author photograph © Jerry Bauer
Book design by J.K. Lambert

www.vintagebooks.com

CONTENTS

CHAPTER I: THERE IS NO "MODERN" WORLD / 3

As future crises arrive in steep waves, our leaders will realize that the world is not "modern" or "postmodern" but only a continuation of the ancient—a world that, despite its technologies, the best Chinese, Greek, and Roman philosophers would have understood, and known how to navigate.

CHAPTER II: CHURCHILL'S *RIVER WAR* / 17

How Churchill's first large historical work, published in 1899, when he was in his twenties, reveals the roots of his thinking and the source of the greatness that enabled him to lead England against Hitler in World War II. The Battle of Omdurman was one of the last of its kind before the age of industrial warfare—a panoramic succession of cavalry charges in which the young Churchill took part. *The River War* shows the ancient world within the modern one: it is here that we start our journey to wrest from the past what we need to arm ourselves for the present.

ment, Machiavelli believes in pagan virtue—ruthless and pragmatic but not amoral. "All armed prophets succeed," he writes, "whereas unarmed ones fail."

caust—that emblematic atrocity—will be hard to apply to our satisfaction. The philosopher Immanuel Kant made it his life's project to define a system of universal laws. Kant's subject is pure integrity, a morality of abstract justice and of intention rather than of consequences. The challenge of realism is to combine tough tactics with long-range Kantian goals in complex and original circumstances.

War will increasingly be unconventional and undeclared and fought within states rather than between them. There have always been warriors who, in Homer's words, "call up the wild joy of war," but the collapse of the Cold War empires and the disorder it engendered—along with the advance of technology and low-end urbanization—has provoked the breakdown of families and the renewal of cults and blood ties. The result is the birth of a new warrior class, as cruel as ever—and better-armed. Defeating warriors will depend on our speed of reaction, not international law.

The Sumerian city-states of the third millennium B.C. in Mesopotamia, the early Mauryan empire of the fourth century B.C. in India, and the early Han empire of the second century B.C. in China are all examples of political systems in which diverse and far-flung territories were tied together through trade and political alliances. Likewise today, in a climate of increasing global trade, the emergence of some kind of loose world governance is probably inevitable—barring a major war between two or more great powers, such as the U.S. and China. But even such a tenuous unity will require the organizing principle of a great power.

True bravery and independence of thought are best anchored by examples from the past. Great leadership will always reside with the mystery of character—one has only to look at the much-maligned Roman emperor Tiberius. In the first half of his rule, Tiberius preserved the institutions and imperial boundaries of his predecessor, Augustus, while leaving them sufficiently stable to survive the excesses of successors like Caligula. He built few cities, annexed few territories, and did not cater to popular whims; rather, he strengthened the territories Rome already possessed by adding military bases, and combined diplomacy with the threat of force to preserve a peace that was favorable to Rome. Unlike Churchill or Pericles, Tiberius is not an inspiring role model. But where his strengths are concerned, he may be a surprisingly good one.

TO CARL D. BRANDT

ACKNOWLEDGMENTS

I thank the following scholars who critiqued early drafts: Francis Fukuyama, Schwarz professor of political economy at Johns Hopkins University; John Gray, professor of European thought at the London School of Economics; David Gress, professor of classics at the Institute of Greek and Latin, Aarhus University, Denmark; Robert B. Strassler, editor of *The Landmark Thucydides;* and in particular, Paul A. Rahe, Jay P. Walker professor of history at the University of Tulsa. However, the opinions stated herein are mine alone, as are the mistakes.

William Whitworth, the editor emeritus of *The Atlantic Monthly,* encouraged in me the notion that a journalist could and should delve into subjects normally reserved for scholars. Cullen Murphy, *The Atlantic's* managing editor, read a draft and offered—as he has for years—elegant criticisms. Michael Kelly, *The Atlantic's* editor, helped by publishing an early synopsis of this book as an article. Michael Lind, my friend and colleague at the New America Foundation, read drafts, and offered ideas and detailed suggestions as to further reading. Adam Garfinkle, the editor of *The National Interest,* agreed to publish an excerpt of the manuscript before publication. Owen Harries, the editor emeritus of *The National Interest,* provided encouragement on the subject of determinism. Anastasia Bakolas, a graduate student in international relations at Columbia University and a reader of ancient Greek, did likewise in regard to Thucydides. Other help came from Robert Berlin, Eric Cohen, Carl Coon, Corby Kummer, Ernest Latham, Toby Lester, Alan Luxenberg, Ralph Peters, Harvey Sicherman, and Nikolai Slywka.

Devon Cross, president of the Donors' Forum on International Affairs, provided key financial help early in my career that enabled me to write my first books on Ethiopia and the Balkans. I could not thank her at the time in print; I take the occasion now to do so.

As with my previous books for over a decade, my literary agent, Carl D. Brandt, was a strategist and friend. Joy de Menil, my editor at Random House, emerged as a serene and tolerant advisor, as well as a technician of books. Jason Epstein at Random House provided extensive notes that helped considerably. Marianne Merola at Brandt & Hochman has masterfully arranged foreign language translations for my books and articles over the years.

Most importantly, this project simply could not have been accomplished without the generous financial support of the New America Foundation in Washington, D.C. Ted Halstead, its president and CEO, gave me an institutional base to the extent that I had not previously enjoyed, while allowing me to work at home in western Massachusetts. He is a young visionary, absolutely unintimidated by controversy. I also thank Steve Clemons, James Fallows, Hannah Fischer, Jill Gravender, Sherle Schwenninger, Gordon Silverstein, and the rest of New America's board, staff, fellows, and interns.

Man's real treasure is the treasure of his mistakes, piled up stone by stone through thousands of years. . . . Breaking the continuity with the past, wanting to begin again, is a lowering of man and a plagiarism of the orangutan. It was a Frenchman, Dupont-White, who around 1860 had the courage to exclaim: "Continuity is one of the rights of man; it is a homage of everything that distinguishes him from the beast."

JOSÉ ORTEGA Y GASSET
Toward a Philosophy of History, 1941

PREFACE

The original sin of any writer is to see the world only from his or her point of view. Objectivity is illusory. As Don Quixote tells Sancho Panza, "This that appears to you as a barber's basin is for me Mambrino's helmet, and something else again to another person." Likewise, the discussions of foreign policy experts reveal how the best minds may disagree about the most elementary details. Many times I have heard the word "inaccurate" used by one expert to challenge something that he believes is an error of fact but which is, in truth, only a different interpretation from his own.

Often, what passes for analysis is merely an expression of one's life experiences applied to a specific issue. From that sin stems another—that of selecting facts and insights to defend a particular vision. To this dilemma there may be no solution.

My own autobiography, therefore, is relevant. I have never taught at a university, been resident full-time at a think tank, or served in government. All those useful experiences I lack. The perspective I offer is based on a different kind of education: that of a quarter-century's work mainly as a reporter overseas. It was the shock of seeing wars, political upheaval, and Third World poverty firsthand that drew me to the classics of philosophy and politics, in the hope of finding explanations for the terrors before my eyes. The books that attracted me most were those that in some way or other helped me understand my own experiences on the ground. The seven years I spent in Greece and extensive travel in Sicily and Tunisia brought me closely into contact with Thucydides' *The Peloponnesian War* and Livy's *The War with Hannibal*. These books provided me with a fresh perspective on my own time and the places I was reporting from.

I cannot hope to match the erudition of those who have spent a lifetime studying the great books. A layman encountering the classics could be compared to a traveler during his first days in a strange country: there are things he will misinterpret, but he will also spot things that longtime residents have ceased to notice. The nineteenth-century explorer Sir Richard Francis Burton writes:

> Despise not, gentle reader, first impressions . . . if a sharp, well-defined outline is to be drawn, it must be done immediately after arrival at a place; when the sense of contrast is still fresh upon the mind, and before second and third have ousted first thoughts. . . . The man who has dwelt a score of years in a place, has forgotten every feeling with which he first sighted it; and if he writes about it, he writes for himself and for his fellow-oldsters, not for the public. The sketcher who acts as I propose to do will, of course, make an occasional bad blunder. . . . But, in the main, the *guâche* will be true and vivid.[1]

Philosophy is as exciting for the layman as it is for the expert, and I hope that I am able to communicate my enthusiasm for the philosophers whose work I explore. My choices are somewhat arbitrary. I can hear a reader thinking, *If he writes about Machiavelli, then why not about Nietzsche; if Kant, why not Locke?* Because my focus is foreign policy, I have emphasized a few philosophers and writers who I believe are especially relevant to and provocative on that subject.

Philosophy is not necessarily instructive. It can be useless or, in some cases, even dangerous: Neville Chamberlain was well-read in the classics, much like Winston Churchill. Benito Mussolini's foreign minister, Count Ciano, was a devotee of Seneca. Martin Heidegger, whom some consider the greatest philosopher of the twentieth century, became a Nazi after Hitler rose to power. But while great dangers exist, one may still try to extract the benefits of philosophy for the sake of policymakers, particularly in regard to subjects that one has firsthand journalistic experience of.

Indeed, in the essay that follows I am still a journalist: I report on the classics and the views of contemporary scholars, integrating them into a story much as any journalist would with the disparate material at hand.

I am not an optimist or an idealist. Americans can afford optimism partly because their institutions, including the Constitution, were conceived by men who thought tragically. Before the first president was sworn in, the rules of impeachment were established. James Madison wrote in *Federalist No. 51* that men are so far beyond redemption that the only solution is to set ambition against ambition, and interest against interest: "If men were angels, no government would be necessary." Our separation of powers is based on that grim view of human behavior. The French Revolution, conversely, began with boundless faith in the good sense of the masses—and in the capacity of intellectuals to engineer good results—and ended with the guillotine.

Our Founders were constructive pessimists to the degree that they worried constantly about what might go wrong in human relations. Just as it is the writer's job to inspire, it can also be his job to disturb—to say what his intended audience would rather not hear. Foreign policy, too, is often conceived in the light of worst-case scenarios. Thus, my pessimism and my skepticism may be germane. For the trials of statesmen in the new century will arise not from the many things that will go right in international relations, and which humanists will duly celebrate, but from the darker issues of this time.

Any discussion of the new century, however, must start with the old one.

WARRIOR POLITICS

CHAPTER I

THERE IS NO

"MODERN" WORLD

The evils of the twentieth century arose from populist movements that were monstrously exploited in the name of utopian ideals, and had their power amplified by new technologies. The Nazi party began as a crusade for workers' rights organized by a Munich locksmith, Anton Drexler, in 1919, before Hitler took it over the following year. The Bolsheviks also emerged amid emancipating political upheaval and, like the Nazis, exploited the dream of social renewal. Once the Nazis and Bolsheviks were in power, the inventions of the Industrial Age became crucial to their crimes. As for Mao Zedong, his push for labor-intensive industrialization, through the establishment of utopian communes, led to the deaths of at least 20 million Chinese during the Great Leap Forward from 1958 to 1962.[1]

The twentieth century may be a poor guide to the twenty-first, but only fools would discount it, particularly because populist movements now permeate the world, provoking disorder and demanding political and economic transformation. Asia is a specific cause for concern. India, Pakistan, China, and other emerging powers pulse with new technologies, nationalistic zeal, and disintegrative forces within. Recall the words of Alexander Hamilton:

> To look for a continuation of harmony between a number of independent, unconnected sovereignties situated in the same neighborhood would be to disregard the uniform course of human events, and to set at defiance the accumulated experience of ages.[2]

Thus, the evils of the twenty-first century may also arise from populist movements, taking advantage of democratization, motivated this time by religious and sectarian beliefs, and empowered by a post–Industrial Revolution: particularly information technology. Hindu extremists who burned down mosques in India in the early 1990s and attacked Christians in the late 1990s belong to a working-class movement within India's democracy that uses videocassettes and the Internet to spread its message. Similar phenomena have occurred in Indonesia, Iran, Nigeria, Algeria, Mexico, Fiji, Egypt, Pakistan, the West Bank, and Arab Nazareth, to name but a few places where religious and ethnic groups, predominantly working-class and inspired by democratization, use modern communications technology to stir unrest.

Populist rage is fueled by social and economic tensions, aggravated often by population growth and resource scarcity in an increasingly urbanized planet. In the coming decades, 2 or 3 billion more people will live in the vast, impoverished cities of the developing world.

Global capitalism will contribute to this peril, smashing traditions and dynamically spawning new ones. The benefits of capitalism are not distributed equitably, so the more dynamic the capitalist expansion, the more unequal the distribution of wealth that usually results.[3] Thus, two dynamic classes will emerge under globalization—the entrepreneurial nouveaux riches and, more ominously, the new subproletariat: the billions of working poor, recently arrived from the countryside, inhabiting the expanding squatters' settlements that surround big cities in Africa, Eurasia, and South America.

It is expected that Internet access through computers and cellular phones will increase from 2.5 percent of the world's population today to 30 percent by 2010; but of the 70 percent of the world still not connected by that date, about half will never have made a phone call.[4] Disparities will be enormous, while the terrorism that arises from such disparities will enjoy unprecedented technological resources.

The spread of information will not necessarily encourage stability. Johannes Gutenberg's invention of movable type in the mid-fifteenth century led not only to the Reformation but to the religious wars that followed it, as the sudden proliferation of texts spurred doctrinal controversies and awakened long-dormant grievances. The spread of information in the coming decades will lead not just to new social compacts, but to new divisions as people discover new and complex issues over which to disagree.

I focus on the dark side of every development not because the future will necessarily be bad, but because that is what foreign policy crises have always been about.

———

Western policymakers, according to their public statements, believe that ethnic and religious unrest is caused by political oppression, even though it is political freedom itself that has often unleashed the violence that liberal societies abhor. There is nothing more volatile and more in need of disciplined, enlightened direction than vast populations of underpaid, underemployed, and badly educated workers divided by ethnicity and beliefs.

Peacemaking, in particular, will become increasingly difficult. That is because successful peace talks require the centralization of power. Only strong rulers can justify the historic about-faces necessary for peace, often with the help of pliant medias and minimal opposition. Without the tools of dictatorship, Anwar Sadat of Egypt and King Hussein of Jordan could not have made peace with Israel. Democratization is a long and uneven process: it will generate weak and uncertain rulers before it generates stable organizations. Some say that only when the Arab world becomes democratic will it make peace with Israel: not necessarily. Liberalization in places like Egypt and Syria may unleash extremist forces that, in the near term, will further destabilize the Middle East.

Western policymakers believe that dictators can be defeated merely by removing them. The nineteenth-century Swiss historian Jacob Burckhardt writes: "Like bad physicians, they thought to cure the disease by removing the symptoms, and fancied that if the tyrant were put to death, freedom would follow of itself."[5] In the 1990s, Western governments demanded elections throughout the developing world, often in places with low literacy rates, weak institutions, and raging ethnic disputes. Dictators were replaced by elected prime ministers. But because the dictators themselves were manifestations of bad social and economic development, their removal frequently permitted the same uncivil practices to continue in democratic clothing; as for example in Pakistan and Côte d'Ivoire, two large bellwether states in South Asia and West Africa, where elected leaders stole vast amounts of money and played one ethnic group against the other, until by the end of the 1990s the military in both countries staged coups, which the local populations greeted with demonstrable relief.[6] Of course, military rule solved nothing, and the unrest continued.

Even when the West intervenes and takes charge of local administration, as in Kosovo and Haiti, intractable cultural and historical factors may preclude stability. On the last day of the twentieth century, six months after President Bill Clinton and British prime minister Tony Blair had declared victory in Kosovo, Bernard Kouchner, the United Nations administrator there, said that ethnic reconciliation between Orthodox Christian Serbs and Moslem Albanians remained a distant goal. "You cannot change the mentality and the heart of a person after centuries of difficulties, fights, hatred, in some weeks and months. It is not possible."[7]

It is not only ethnic reconciliation and the triumph of liberal democracy that should not be taken for granted; neither should the present system of nation-states. The postcolonial era is only in the early phases of collapse. The residue of European empires in Africa and the Asian subcontinent still provides a somewhat stable division of territories. Only in marginal areas such as Somalia and Sierra Leone has that system broken down. In the next decade, it may crumble further in much larger, more populous, and more urbanized societies—for example Nigeria and Pakistan, where intervention scenarios will be particularly problematic.

The dramatic growth of cities in recent decades raises the possibility that in the new century vast metroplexes, with their own adjacent hinterlands and loyal populations, will overshadow nations in political importance. The United States is increasingly a conglomeration of peacefully competing city-states. Eighty-five percent of Arizona's inhabitants live in the Greater Tucson–Phoenix urban corridor; in 2050 it is estimated that 98 percent will.[8] The Pacific Northwest is becoming a single urban community located along Interstate 5, or "I-5 Main Street" as locals call it, from Eugene, Oregon, to Vancouver, British Columbia, increasingly oblivious of the U.S.–Canada border. Overseas, a significant number of emerging city-states—São Paulo, Bogotá, Moscow, Kiev, Baku, and Kunming in south China—that are surrounded by weak and anarchic regions, may be controlled by corporate and military oligarchs: some enlightened, others criminal. In such high-tech, neomedieval principalities, money may buy elections and militaries and security services may influence policy, in degrees far greater and subtler than today.

In the wealthiest parts of the world, where the rule of law exists, it is not clear if such emerging political entities will need governments at all: some may survive on nimble executive branches that provide a few essential services while increasingly robust global institutions take over other bureaucratic responsibilities.

Cities have always lived beyond Good and Evil, in splendor and ugliness, creativity and terror, with new ideas and gadgets: places to be experienced rather than judged. Imagine the multitudes of wealthy city-states in years hence: happy in their concrete beehives, subsisting on cinema, television, and the Internet, drifting from one craze to the next, conditioned to such a degree by the opinions of others through ever-expanding electronic media that their individuality becomes imperiled, even as they loudly proclaim otherwise.[9] Only the Islamic masses have seriously questioned the moral status of cities in our era. Islamic fundamentalism gives moral and psychological support to millions of peasants who have migrated into Middle Eastern, South Asian, and Indonesian cities, where in poor outlying slums their values are under attack, as water systems and other basic services break down. Thus, while our elites babble about globalism as they once did about Marxism, new class struggles arise, tied to religion and the tensions of Third World urban life. The twentieth century was the last in history when humankind was mostly rural.[10] The battlefields of the future will be highly complex urban terrains. If our soldiers cannot fight and kill at close range, our status as a superpower is in question.

The Industrial Revolution was about scale: vast factory complexes, skyscrapers, and railway grids concentrating power in the hands of rulers of large territories: not only responsible rulers such as Bismarck and Disraeli, but Hitler and Stalin, too, intensifying their evils. But the post–Industrial Revolution empowers anyone with a cellular phone and a bag of explosives. America's military superiority guarantees that such new adversaries will not fight according to our notions of fairness: they will come at us by surprise, asymmetrically, at our weakest points, as they often have in the past.

Asymmetry gives terrorists and cybercriminals their strength, since such adversaries operate beyond accepted international norms and value systems on a plane where atrocity is a legitimate form of war.[11] The enormous size of our democratic institutions makes military planning and weapons procurement both cumbersome and publicly accountable. Our future adversaries will be under no such restrictions. Their operations will be fast and simple, leaving no paper trails and incurring no public oversight: that will be their advantage. Foolish dictators like Saddam Hussein who fight conventional wars against us are historically rare: more likely is a chemical and biological version of Pearl Harbor.

Biological weapons will become increasingly available to terrorist groups. Even if such weapons were to remain within the hands of states, diplomacy may not be enough to neutralize them, since they are part of an ongoing, unstoppable biotech revolution. Indeed, the acceleration of technology in genetics, biology, chemistry, optics, and computer sciences provides immense new vistas for uncontrolled weaponry.

Consider, too, that we are at the brink of a major new expansion in space exploration and satellite deployment. By some estimates, 20 percent of the U.S. economy may be devoted to space-related activities by 2025, with software programmers, engineers, and other highly skilled workers lured from around the world (particularly from the Indian subcontinent) to develop and manage these new technologies for U.S.–based multinationals.[12] The diffusion of such power to private boardrooms may unleash new evils, yet unnamed: recall that the words "fascism," "totalitarianism," and "Nazism" did not acquire common currency until the third and fourth decades of the last century.

Then again, technology could magnify the power of states themselves—something else to beware of, given our experience of the last hundred years. For example, a rogue state could employ new technologies to wage an undeclared war against the United

States, through the strategic use of terrorists and crime groups, all the while manipulating a powerful global media to conceal its intentions.

Of course, new technologies will bring a host of beneficial developments, but that is another reason for our military and civilian leaders to be cautious. Scientific optimism at the beginning of the twentieth century left Europeans unprepared for the calamities that would soon befall them. New devices will provide new opportunities, as they always have, for human mischief. Unlike a sword or an ax, which acts as an extension of the human arm, the machine bears no relation to the body; thus, it breaks forever the emotional link between a violent act and its perpetrator, greatly expanding the scope of impersonal viciousness. Consider the assault rifle, a machine that converts heat energy into kinetic energy. For that is another lesson of the twentieth century: the link—when we are not vigilant—between technological acceleration and barbarism.

So far I have mentioned only *driving forces:* trends that are already visible (the expansion of populations, cities, capitalism, technology, income divides, and so on). But there will also be *sideswipes:* developments that come at us by surprise, as AIDS did in the 1980s.[13] Natural disasters like floods and earthquakes, which destabilize fragile political systems, may be one such *sideswipe:* the cloning of human beings who are genetically engineered for military purposes by a rising power such as China may be another. Then there is global warming, which could turn out to be both a *driving force* and a *sideswipe,* by precipitating both natural disasters and extremist political reactions to them.

—

The very word "modern" suggests a desire to separate our life and times from the past.[14] "Modern" ideas, politics, architecture, music, and so on imply not an extension of the past or even a reaction against it, but a rejection of it. The term "modern" is a celebration of *Progress*. Yet the more "modern" we and our technologies become—the more our lives become mechanized and abstract—the more our instincts are likely to rebel, and the more cunning and perverse we are likely to become, however subtly.

Electronic communications, by allowing us to avoid face-to-face encounters, make cruelty easier to accomplish, as we enter an abstract realm of pure strategy and deception carrying few psychological risks. Auschwitz was possible partly because new industrial technology distanced the German perpetrators from their acts. An executive at a leading Internet company told me that the most brutal corporate power plays—in which whole departments are "downsized," while each unit is kept ignorant of what the others are undergoing—occur at firms where electronic communications have replaced face-to-face dealings.

Meritocracy also fuels aggression, because it creates new opportunities for millions venting their ambitions—putting them in desperate competition with each other. We see this plainly in the workplace and in the highest reaches of business, government, and the media. Therefore, to expect future relations among states and other political groups to be more harmonious, or wiser, because of technological advances seems unrealistic.

In those cultures that fail to compete technologically, many young males may, like warriors, rape and pillage in almost ritual style, wearing tribal insignia rather than uniforms, like Serb and Albanian paramilitaries, Indonesian militiamen, Moslem holy fighters in Kashmir, Chechen brigands, and Russian soldiers. Of course, places such as Russia and Serbia may recover politically and economically, and their young men may become industrious. Such blighted places will never form a majority of countries, but will remain a periodically shifting minority—sufficient to create regional instability and constant crises with which statesmen must deal. The media cliché "the global village" confers prestige on the very media which employs it; witness CNN. But statesmen must grapple with difficult truths, not clichés. Conflict and community are both inherent in the human condition. While the postindustrial West seeks to deny the persistence of conflict, Africa, Asia, the Indian subcontinent, and the Caucasus, among other places, demonstrate its survival, as ethnic and religious groups seek to dominate rivals and create their own dominions by toppling existing elites.[15]

It takes a shallow grasp of history to believe that solutions exist to most international problems. Often there are no solutions, only confusion and unsatisfactory choices.

That is why when General George Marshall—the architect of America's World War II military victory and the postwar rebuilding of Europe—became head of the Infantry School at Fort Benning, Georgia, in 1927, he discarded the rule book with its emphasis on "solutions," and replaced it with "realistic exercises," which trained officers for "initiative" and "judgment."[16] The rule book for incoming presidents and secretaries of state must reflect Marshall's wisdom at Fort Benning. Marshall doubted

> whether a man can think with full wisdom and with deep convictions regarding . . . the basic international issues today who

has not at least reviewed in his mind the period of the Peloponnesian War and the Fall of Athens.[17]

Marshall knew ancient history. Likewise, any new rules for leadership will have to reflect upon it. Ancient history, as I will demonstrate, is the surest guide to what we are likely to face in the early decades of the twenty-first century.

This is not an essay about what to think: but about how to think. I am not writing about specific policy but about policy as an outgrowth of thinking—not feeling. Seasoned policymakers like Marshall were not guided by sympathy but by necessity and self-interest. The Marshall Plan was not a gift to Europe but an effort to contain Soviet expansion; when necessity and self-interest are properly calculated, history calls such thinking "heroic."

In the opinion of Marshall, a courtly and aloof officer whom few dared call by his first name, heroism was the result of cool judgment reached on the basis of inadequate information: on a real battlefield, information about the enemy is always incomplete; by the time enough is known, it is too late to do anything.

Foreign policy crises are like battles. Domestic policy tends to emerge from statistical studies and drawn-out negotiations between the executive and legislative branches, but foreign policy frequently relies on sheer intuition to fathom the often violent, fast-moving events overseas, complicated by cultural differences. In a world in which democracy and technology are developing faster than are the institutions needed to sustain them—even as states themselves are eroding and being transformed beyond recognition by urbanization and the information age—foreign policy will be the art, rather than the science, of permanent crisis management.

As future crises arrive in steep waves, our leaders will realize that the world is not "modern" or "postmodern," but only a continuation of the "ancient": a world that, despite its technologies, the best Chinese, Greek, and Roman philosophers might have been able to cope with. So, too, would those like General Marshall, who manifest the ancient tradition of skepticism and constructive realism.

But skepticism and realism are categories far too broad to form a useful guide for statesmen.

After all, both Winston Churchill and Neville Chamberlain were realists, calculating possibilities and outcomes based on past experience and self-interest. Churchill's respect for restoring the European balance of power in England's favor needs no belaboring. But the appeasers, too, were pragmatists. German rearmament was, historically speaking, normal, and in the mid-1930s Hitler could have been seen as simply another contemptible dictator with whom the West had to deal, rather than as the self-described maniac of *Mein Kampf*—especially since two decades earlier, 8.5 million men had died in a war born of miscalculation and confusion that produced no demonstrable gain. Far from it; it produced a disaster. Stalin, on the other hand, had already proven himself a mass murderer, while Hitler (prior to the outbreak of World War II at least) had not. For the appeasers, permitting a rearmed Germany to check Soviet Russia seemed perfectly reasonable.

Yet that did not stop Churchill from seeking not only to contain

Hitler but, ultimately, to destroy him. It did not stop Churchill from fearing Germany more than Soviet Russia, even though it had been Churchill who, as British secretary of war from 1919 to 1921, led the Western effort to topple the Bolsheviks in the civil war following the October Revolution. Indeed, Churchill—who sought an alliance with Stalin against Hitler—had always been more fiercely anti-Communist than any of the appeasers.

So the question arises: how was Churchill a realist in a way that Chamberlain was not? What did Churchill seem to know, in that particular circumstance, that can guide statesmen in future crises? Answering those questions is the first step toward confronting the world before us.

CHAPTER II

CHURCHILL'S *RIVER WAR*

The British historian John Keegan writes: "No other citizen of the last century of the second millennium, the worst in history, deserved better to be recognized as a hero to mankind" than Churchill. Both Churchill and Franklin Delano Roosevelt, Keegan says, "derived their moral purpose from the Anglo-Saxon tradition of the rule of law and freedom of the individual. Each could champion that tradition because the sea protected his country from the landbound enemies of liberty."[1]

On June 4, 1940, before the House of Commons, following the British evacuation from Dunkirk and with France close to defeat, Churchill told his people: "We shall defend our island, whatever the cost may be. We shall fight on the landing-grounds; we shall fight in the fields and in the streets.... We shall never surrender." Rarely have a few phrases so inspired a nation. The Oxford philosopher Isaiah Berlin remarked that Churchill "idealised" his countrymen "with such intensity that in the end they approached his ideal and began to see themselves as he saw them...."[2]

There are many ways to explain Churchill's power and greatness, but Berlin may have come closest when he wrote: "Churchill's dominant category, the single, central, organising principle of his moral and intellectual universe, is a historical imagination so strong, so comprehensive, as to encase the whole of the present and the whole of the future in a framework of a rich and multicoloured past." And because Churchill's "strongest sense is the sense of the past," particularly ancient history, he is also, Berlin explains, "acquainted with the darkness. . . ."

Churchill saw through Hitler early on, because Churchill was familiar with monsters to a degree that Chamberlain was not. Chamberlain's was a shallow realism. He knew his people wanted peace, and their money spent on domestic needs rather than on armaments, so he gave them those things. (When Chamberlain returned from Munich after appeasing Hitler, he was proclaimed a hero.) But Churchill knew more. He was a man with fewer illusions, partly because he had spent much of his life—beyond his school years—reading and writing about history and experiencing Britain's colonial wars firsthand as a soldier and journalist. Thus, he knew how intractable and irrational human beings were. Like all wise men, he thought tragically: for we create moral standards in order to measure our own inadequacies.

Of course, Churchill was far from perfect, especially in regard to his policy toward Hitler. Nor may Chamberlain have been as much of a dupe as many suppose. Had events worked out even slightly differently, Chamberlain might be held in higher esteem now. Chamberlain may have been more unlucky than unwise. Building up Britain's defenses while testing Hitler's intentions, as Chamberlain did, had the virtue of gaining Britain time while uniting public opinion behind the government for the eventual fight against

Hitler. Still, there is something that we can label Churchillian that is worth exploring as an ideal.

It is a long way from Europe at the start of World War II to the parched deserts of Sudan in the late nineteenth century. But it is there that Churchill's thinking is revealed on issues that we face today. It is there that we start our journey to wrest from the past what we need to arm ourselves for the present.

In the mid-1980s, I was in Khartoum, the Sudanese capital, covering a famine that had engulfed the Horn of Africa. In Khartoum I came across a book about the Sudan of a hundred years before: *The River War: An Historical Account of the Re-Conquest of the Soudan.* It was Churchill's first large historical work, published in 1899 in two volumes.[3]

The River War is about two decades in British colonial history, beginning in 1881, when Britain intervened militarily in Egypt to keep its ruler, Tewfik Pasha, on the throne after a popular revolt. Britain's naval bombardment of Alexandria, followed by a successful troop landing, had left it with the task of governing both Egypt and Sudan, the latter an Egyptian province. The same year, the Islamic rebellion of Mohammed Ahmed—called the "Mahdi," or Savior—plunged Sudan's remote deserts into turmoil. Britain sent General Charles George Gordon, a decorated war hero, to evacuate the Egyptian garrison in Khartoum. There the Mahdi's forces surrounded Gordon, who withstood months of siege before Britain's prime minister, William Gladstone, belatedly dispatched a rescue mission that reached the city two days after Gordon, sword in hand, was killed by Mahdist warriors. The debacle contributed to the liberal government's collapse and the beginning of a long period of conservative rule in Britain. The conservatives began the process of reconquering Sudan that included the infiltration of spies, the extension of a railway south along the Nile, and the dispatch of an expeditionary force. It culminated in General Herbert Kitchener's victory over the Mahdist army in 1898 at Omdurman, on the left bank of the Nile, opposite Khartoum. The Battle of Omdurman was one of the last of its kind before the age of industrial war: a panoramic succession of cavalry charges in which the young Churchill, an officer in the 21st Lancers, took part. Dramatic youthful memories such as these may have given Churchill a larger vision of Britain's destiny than what Chamberlain had.

Churchill's *River War*, with its sweeping descriptions of "civilisation" and "barbarism," its uncomfortable judgments about the customs of other nations and peoples, and its quaint and pictorial scenes of battle, reads like Herodotus's *History* and sometimes even like Homer's *Iliad*. The same man who would save Western civilization four decades later writes about "brave and honest . . . negroes as black as coal" who "displayed the virtues of barbarism." He describes the Arabs as the "stronger race" that "imposed its customs and language on the negroes. . . . The Egyptian was strong, patient, healthy, and docile. The negro was in all these respects his inferior."[4] Still, for Churchill, Egyptian rule "was not kindly, wise, or profitable. Its aim was to exploit, not to improve the local population": it substituted "the rough justice of the sword" with "the intricacies of corruption and bribery." Churchill's claim that "the fertile soil and enervating climate of the [Nile] Delta" failed to produce "a warrior race" is the epitome of geographical fatalism—or "determinism" in the language of scholars—and thus regrettable by the standards of contemporary opinion.

There is also Churchill the travel writer describing the "filmy" desert air that "glittered and shimmered as over a furnace"; the *khors* (rocky ditches) "filled with a strange, sweet-scented grass"; the "bristle of bayonets" to the "wild and thrilling accompaniment" of the "drums and fifes of the English regiments." At the Battle of Omdurman, the Mahdist army, its banners decorated with Koranic writing, reminds the young Churchill of the "old representations of the Crusaders in the Bayeux tapestry."[5]

Churchill always craved drama and scenery—elements that contributed to the power of his wartime speeches. He is like a geographer for whom human beings are the intelligent fauna of a landscape. He patiently explains the interrelationships of rainfall, soil fertility, climate, elephants, birds, antelopes, and nomadic tribes. Churchill is not racist: he is concerned with cultural rather than biological differences. He claims that the huge area of the Sudan "contains many differences of climate and situation, and these have produced peculiar and diverse breeds of men."[6] It is an approach similar to that of Aristotle, Montesquieu, Gibbon, Toynbee, and other great philosophers and historians.

What saves *The River War* from both fatalism and mere romance is that the harshly realistic portrayal of tribes and desert makes their conquest all the more significant and inspiring: an intractable physical and human landscape becomes the obstacle that moral men surmount. The more hopeless the history and geography appear to be and the more unpromising the human material, the more prolific the opportunities for heroism. For it is individual men and women, as well as geography, who determine history. As Isaiah Berlin writes, referring to ancient Greece: history is " 'what Alcibiades did and suffered,' " despite "all the efforts of the social

sciences" to prove otherwise. *The River War* lives up to that defini-
tion. It is a narrative that gives personal genius its full due. Take
General Gordon, about whom Churchill writes:

> One day he was a subaltern of sappers; on another he com-
> manded the Chinese army; the next he directed an orphanage;
> or was Governor-General of the Soudan, with supreme powers
> of life and death and peace and war. But in whatever capacity . . .
> we perceive a man careless alike of the frowns of men or the
> smiles of women, of life or comfort, wealth or fame.[7]

Gordon had first distinguished himself through his reckless
bravery in the Crimean War. After burning the Chinese emperor's
palace and helping suppress the Taiping uprising, he returned tri-
umphantly to England in 1865, where he was dubbed Chinese Gordon. In the 1870s we find him in Equatoria, in southern Sudan,
where he mapped the upper Nile and established a string of colonial stations. Later as governor-general of the Sudan, he crushed
rebellions and fought the slave trade. A devout Christian, he was a
martyr-in-waiting by the time he made his last stand against
Mahdist forces in Khartoum. As with Plutarch's portrayal of great
men, Churchill's portrayal of Gordon shows that he is principally
concerned with personalities and individual action; duty per-
formed and rewarded.[8]

For Churchill, glory is rooted in a morality of consequence: of
actual results rather than good intentions. The British military enterprise in the Nile Valley was admirable only because it was followed by "the marvellous work of creating good government and
prosperity."[9] The British did, in fact, build roads and other infrastructure, and developed public services. On many visits to Sudan

in the 1980s, I heard Sudanese recall with pride and nostalgia the long period of British rule and the decade of independence afterward—before unrest, rebellion, and religious fanaticism returned for the first time since the Mahdi.

Churchill may at times have been naïve about Britain's long-lasting effect upon its colonies, but he was never cynical. Indeed, at a time when the newly instituted democratic government of Sierra Leone pleads with Britain not to withdraw its commandos; when the international community maintains protectorates in Bosnia and Kosovo to prevent a resurgence of ethnic genocide; when an Australian occupation force helps safeguard human rights in East Timor, it is difficult to condemn Churchill for having supported colonialist interventions that provided stability and a better material life for the local inhabitants. The fact is that Churchill's rhetoric and some of his intentions are strikingly similar to those of today's moral interventionists.

Churchill writes that British colonialism in the Nile Valley was honorable because it aimed

> to give peace to warring tribes, to administer justice where all was violence, to strike the chains off the slave, to draw the richness from the soil, to plant the earliest seeds of commerce and learning, to increase in whole peoples their capacities for pleasure and diminish their chances of pain—what more beautiful idea or more valuable reward can inspire human effort? The act is virtuous, the exercise invigorating, and the result often extremely profitable.[10]

When the West contemplated intervening in the former Yugoslavia and elsewhere, it too sought to replace violence with justice, to end human indignities, to lay the groundwork for commercial renewal, and so forth. Of course, the West was not seeking profit or "to draw the richness from the soil," as were Churchill and other British colonialists. Nor did the West harbor a racist view of the local inhabitants of the kind that the British did.

Moreover, to a greater extent than advocates of moral intervention in the 1990s, Churchill was alert to the practical consequences as well as the moral benefits of military enterprises. He shows how the defeat of the Italians in 1896 in Ethiopia might inspire Islamic fundamentalists to attack pro-British Egyptian garrisons next door in Sudan. Thus, restoring the balance of power in northeastern Africa was a key reason for General Kitchener's expedition.[11] It was an expedition that Britain could afford, because it was otherwise at peace and its economy was prosperous. Britain was among the leading manufacturing nations and financial centers of the day. And that may be the most tantalizing similarity between Britain's intervention in Sudan and ours in the Balkans: in the 1990s, we were a nation at peace enjoying the easy dominance that followed our victory in the Cold War. Thus, we could afford a moral enterprise whose strategic benefits are still being debated.

In his mid-twenties, Churchill doesn't delude himself about local realities. He is aware of the faults of Britain's allies in Egypt to a degree that many Americans in South Vietnam in the 1960s were not. He explains that Egyptian oppression, rather than religious fanaticism, was the real cause of the Mahdi's revolt. The Sudanese, he says, were "being ruined; their property was plundered; their women were ravished; their liberties were curtailed. . . ."[12] Nor is Churchill blind to Gordon's faults, however much he admires the martyred general. He compares Gordon's Christian mysticism and unstable personality to Mahdi fanaticism.

But Churchill's skepticism never leads to despair. He favors military action—provided that it is worthwhile, morally and strategically; that it is within his country's capacity; and that there are no illusions regarding the obstacles: the climate, the vast distances, the warring local factions, and the general underdevelopment of the country.

Churchill showed again that he was a man without illusions when he urged the United States to delay, from 1942 to 1944, a cross-Channel operation against German-occupied Europe: his soaring optimism, necessary to rally England in the dark days of 1940, quickly turned to caution the moment America entered the war. Four decades earlier in the Sudan, Churchill had written about how the slow, methodical buildup against the Mahdists in the late 1880s and 1890s ensured a subsequent British victory. His patience and restraint bridge the gap between realism and idealism. The realist may have the same goals as the idealist, but he understands that action must sometimes be delayed to ensure success.

Churchill the arch-colonialist is inseparable from the Churchill who stood alone against Hitler. The striking, passionate, rhythmic language that inspired millions listening to him over the radio in 1940 is everywhere present in the pages of *The River War*. Both in the 1890s and fifty years later, Churchill's unapologetic warmongering arose not from a preference for war, but from a breastbeating Victorian sense of imperial destiny—amplified by what Isaiah Berlin calls a rich historical imagination. In a brilliant analysis of *The River War*, the American scholar Paul A. Rahe likens the twenty-five-year-old Churchill's style and worldview to that of the ancient Greek and Roman historians.[13] Churchill knows that if a nation is to prosper, it must always have something to fight for:

> For, as in the Roman State, when there are no more worlds to conquer and no rivals to destroy, nations exchange the desire for power for the love of art, and so by a gradual, yet continual, enervation and decline turn from the vigorous beauties of the nude to the more subtle allurements of the draped, and then sink to actual eroticism and ultimate decay.[14]

The man who celebrated his nation's colonialist enterprise and later roused it to war against a much stronger Germany was deeply immersed not only in the history of his own country and civilization, but also in ancient history: which teaches that without struggle—and the sense of insecurity that motivates it—there is decadence. In the first century B.C., Sallust writes: "The division of the Roman state into warring factions . . . had originated some years before, as a result of peace and of that material prosperity which men regard as the greatest blessing," for "the favourite vices of prosperity" are "licence and pride. . . ."[15] Churchill's understanding of that helps account for his toughness, what the Greeks associated with "manhood" and the "heroic outlook."[16]

The River War and Churchill's World War II speeches are all examples of a particular kind of hardheadedness—the ability to establish moral priorities. The appeasers found it morally repugnant to seek an alliance with Stalin or to support a military coup against Hitler, since he had come to power democratically, notwithstanding postelection backroom deals. The appeasers, writes Professor Rahe, indulged their moral sensitivities at a terrible cost; "they were more nice than wise. In refusing to commit the smaller sin, they incurred a far greater wrong."

Today, unlike in the late 1930s, we face no threat on the scale of Hitler. The bipolar nature of World War II and Cold War alliances is no longer evident. Our situation is more similar to that of the late Victorians, who had to deal with nasty little wars in anarchic corners of the globe, such as Sudan.[17] Is it too far-fetched to imagine our own expedition through similar desert wastes to apprehend another Mahdi-like figure, Osama bin Laden? *The River War* shows the ancient world within the modern one. It shows that only by accepting geography and the long record of history is it possible to move beyond them: such constraining forces should be overcome, not denied. Thus, a Churchillian approach to foreign policy starts with humility, with seeing how the struggles of today are strikingly similar to those of antiquity.

CHAPTER III

LIVY'S PUNIC WAR

Of course, the ancient world was different from our own. Herodotus records customs and atrocities that, while strange and shocking to us, were commonplace 2,500 years ago: the Issedones of Central Asia, who chopped up the bones of the dead and mixed them with those of sheep; the Scythians, who cut the throats of sacrificial victims over a bowl, then dismembered them and threw the hacked-off joints into the air; the Trausi of Thrace, who mourned the birth of a baby because of the suffering it would endure through life and rejoiced at funerals because the pain of existence had ended; the Persians, who took the best-looking male children of their subject populations and castrated them, while burying others alive. Herodotus may have exaggerated these horrors or even invented some, but in his age cruelty was routine and usually went unremarked upon, just as in subsequent epochs gladiators fought to the death, Christians were thrown to starving lions, and so on.

The differences between past and present need not be further belabored. Nevertheless, the resemblances with our times are eerie, because human passions and motivations have changed little over the millennia. Knowledge about ancient times helps us understand our own: "nothing is great or little, otherwise than by comparison," writes Jonathan Swift.[1] In his masterpiece, *Gulliver's Travels*, the giants of Brobdingnag allow Gulliver to see far beyond the conceit of his own civilization, while the tiny inhabitants of Lilliput—caricatures of modern men—"see with great exactness, but at no great distance."[2]

To listen to public discourse in America, one would think that morality is entirely a Judeo-Christian invention. But it was the pagan writer Plutarch's main theme in his profiles of great men.[3] Comparing Alcibiades, a Greek politician, with Coriolanus, a Roman general, Plutarch notes that to maintain power "by terror, violence, and oppression is not a disgrace only, but an injustice."[4] When Seneca rails against leaders who display anger, it is because many of the states with which he was familiar had weak or nonexistent institutions that could not restrain their rulers—like some states in the developing world today.[5]

And when Cicero says in the first century B.C. that "the whole foundation of the human community" is threatened by treating foreigners worse than fellow Romans, he already lays the basis for international society.[6] Times have changed less than we think.

Few writers were more concerned with morality and the effect that individual men have on events than Livy, the historian of the early and middle Roman Republic. And few works demonstrate the un-

canny resemblance between the ancient world and the recently departed twentieth century as much as Livy's *The War with Hannibal*,
a cautionary tale with many resemblances to World War II that
seems to warn against the hubris of our own era.[7]

Like previous generations, baby boomers believe in their singu-
larity: that their times are unique and that they are wiser and more
enlightened than those who preceded them. Livy exhorts against
this perennial self-regard while showing how common it has been.
When a Carthaginian general fails to convince his countrymen that
their good fortune cannot last forever, Livy notes wryly that "it is
only human nature to refuse, in a time of rejoicing, to listen to arguments which would turn the substance of it to a shadow."[8]

Livy (Titus Livius) was born in Patavium (Padua) in 59 B.C. and
died in Rome in 17 A.D. He devoted half his life to writing a long
history of Rome, consisting of 142 books, of which *The War with
Hannibal* comprises books 21 to 30.[9] Livy took no part in politics
and consequently had no inside knowledge at his disposal. Nor was
he closely involved with the literary world of his time, which included the poets Horace and Virgil. Unlike them, he mistrusted the
prosperity of his age, considering its decadence the beginning of
Rome's decline. Indeed, while Horace issued triumphalist prophe-
cies of worldwide dominion and Virgil occasionally fawned over
Augustus, Livy noted the dangers that lurked over the horizon
which his fellow Romans preferred to ignore.[10] Livy, the quintes-
sential outsider, is still read because of his colorful descriptions of
men and events and his arresting insights into human nature.

The War with Hannibal shows an ancient version of patriotism:
pride in one's country, its banners and insignias, and its storied
past. Reading Livy, one understands why displaying the flag on

Memorial Day and the Fourth of July is a virtuous act and why national pride is a prerequisite for a Churchillian foreign policy.

Livy's various books provide canonical images of patriotic virtue and extreme sacrifice. Lucius Junius Brutus, the late-sixth-century B.C. Roman commander who overthrew the Etruscan kings, presides over the execution of his own sons for treason. Gaius Mucius Scaevola, another Roman commander, lays his hand on a burning altar to show the Etruscans he will bear any pain to defeat them.[11] And there is Livy's famous description of Lucius Quinctius Cincinnatus, who, in 458 B.C., was "called from his plough" to take reinforcements to a besieged Roman army.[12] Cincinnatus was elected dictator because of his exploits, but as soon as the military emergency was over, he resigned his office. In Livy's account, when Cincinnatus puts on a toga and crosses the Tiber River away from his farm, he symbolically sacrifices his family for the larger good of the republic, putting his wealth in jeopardy for the sake of his country.[13] His return to the farm afterward shows that power is less important to him than the welfare of his family, once his country is no longer in danger. No matter how much Livy embellishes the story, his values are ones we can identify with. Like Alexis de Tocqueville, he understands that healthy republics grow out of strong civic and family ties.

Livy's factual errors and romantic view of the Roman Republic should not dissuade us from his larger truths. It bears repeating that the classics are not read for their factual minutiae but for the way they help us think about our own age. We need to recover the allure that the classics held for nineteenth-century schoolboys like Churchill, who read them not as critics or fact checkers but for their inspiration—and because they had to.

In fact, Livy's belief in Rome's civility is less romantic than it seems. It is based on the solid achievement of a constitutional government: regardless of the stresses of war, annual elections and censuses were held, levies for the army were organized, and claims for exemption were given a fair hearing.[14]

The First Punic War began with a local quarrel between Roman and Greek colonists in Syracuse that, magnified by entangling alliances, brought Rome and Carthage into conflict over the whole of Sicily. It ended with the defeat of Carthage, upon which Rome imposed a crushing and humiliating indemnity. As in Europe in the twentieth century, this led to a second conflict. *The War with Hannibal* is the story of the Second Punic War, which went on without pause for seventeen years in Europe and North Africa until 202 B.C.—a series of great battles that ruined much of the Mediterranean region. Rome's victory in the Second Punic War, like America's in World War II, made it a universal power.

Livy begins his account by calling the Second Punic War "the most memorable war in history...."[15] It would not be an exaggeration to call it one of the greatest wars of all time. The fighting engulfed what in the West was considered the known world.

Livy has been accused of romanticizing Hannibal, the Carthaginian commander. But a first-time reader may see something else: that Livy's Hannibal—in his nihilistic craving for violence and turmoil—has elements of a pre–technological era Hitler. Even by the standards of his time, Hannibal was heartless: he confiscated land and burned children alive for no reason other than the fact of conquest. Hannibal is a falsely heroic leader; he requires continuous war to legitimize his rule and satisfy his own death wish.[16] Like Hitler, he was embittered by the imposed and unjust peace of a previous war. Alas, Hannibal blames his own people rather than himself for his defeat, implying that the Carthaginians aren't sufficiently worthy of him.

Hannibal had the advantage of attacking an enemy morally exhausted from a previous war. As with our Congress—which remained inert while Hitler violated the Treaty of Versailles, entered the Rhineland, and attacked Poland—the Roman Senate had great difficulty dealing with Hannibal's threat: after he had violated the treaty ending the First Punic War and seized Roman territory in Spain.[17] "The Romans looked away, then they took actions that were inadequate for their purpose," writes Yale professor Donald Kagan, comparing the origins of the Second Punic War with those of World War II.[18] Appeasement was alive in the Roman Senate: Roseveltian aristocrats warned of the dangers that Carthage embodied, while isolationist provincials resisted action. As Hannibal pressed toward Rome after marching east from Spain and then crossing the Alps into Italy, the populist and isolationist tribune Quintus Baebius Herennius told the Senate that it was only the nobility that wanted war. By the time the Senate realized it had to act, total war was the only recourse.

In 216 B.C., with "nearly the whole of Italy overrun" and tens of thousands of Roman soldiers killed by Hannibal at the Battle of Cannae in southeastern Italy, Rome's situation resembled England's after Dunkirk and before the Battle of Britain.[19] "It was unparalleled in history . . . what Rome had now to face," Livy writes, in words that foreshadow Churchill's.[20] Like Churchill's England, Rome refused to sue for peace, and fought on.

Rome's limited democracy was a disadvantage over the short term. Its constitution gave military command to two elected leaders for a year at a time only, often leading to incompetent generalship.[21] Moreover, the Roman state could not always compel the population to do what was necessary to defeat Hannibal. Angry arguments between the authorities and suffering villages throughout Italy were frequent. Yet it was Rome's liberal treatment of these same subject villages—something new in Mediterranean history—that ultimately kept them from revolting.[22] Over the long run, it was democracy—however much a pale shadow of our own—that made Rome a nation to a degree that Carthage was not. Livy, quoting the Roman consul Varro, says Carthage's was a "barbarous soldiery," because its troops "know nothing of civilization under law. . . ."[23]

Carthage's army was composed of mercenaries speaking many languages with whom Hannibal could communicate only through interpreters. Its lack of a common purpose contributed to Carthage's defeat. Ironically, Rome's many internal political debates gave it a latent stability, anticipating Machiavelli's assertion that successful states require a modest degree of turmoil to foster a healthy political dynamism.

Rome's war against Hannibal necessitated the Roman equivalent of America's World War II and Cold War executive presidency. The Roman Senate—a prestigious oligarchy—ruled as a supreme war council, while the elected assemblies saw their power wither.[24] The Senate recognized the Carthaginian threat in time, yet preceded with caution while the Roman population, once so passive at Hannibal's victories in Spain, now demanded vengeance against him. Livy tells us that the "wise delaying tactics" of consul Quintus

Fabius Maximus broke "the terrible continuity of Roman defeats," making Hannibal fear that Rome had at last chosen a capable war leader. But in Rome itself, Fabius's actions "met with nothing but contempt."[25] Livy, quoting Fabius, says: "Never mind if they call your caution timidity, your wisdom sloth, your generalship weakness; it is better that a wise enemy should fear you than that foolish friends should praise."[26] Thus, Livy reminds us how public opinion—the clamoring judgments of those around you—can often be wrong.

Is Livy's Hannibal real? Even Livy's detractors admit that he had an uncommon feel for personalities and their influence on events. While he may have been a bit of a romantic popularizer, Livy's view may also represent how Romans of the Augustan age saw their past and their enemies. Indeed, were it not for Livy (and Cicero, too), it is doubtful that republicanism would have survived as an ideal in Rome, even though it was not re-established in practice.

The difference between the Rome of Livy's lifetime and the Rome at the time of the Second Punic War, over two hundred years earlier, approximates the difference between America during the Cold War era and the time of World War II. In Livy's lifetime, Rome saw the decline of small farms, the drift of the population to towns and suburbs, the emergence of a plutocracy in a more complex and affluent society, and revolts against both higher taxes and military service, while the Rome of the Second Punic War had been a time of relative unity and patriotism against a great enemy.

Livy's story blends pride and nostalgia, much as current books celebrate the generation of World War II. As Rome's envoys make their way into the Forum to announce to a cheering, tearful populace that a Carthaginian army has been destroyed near Sena, in northeastern Italy, and that the Carthaginian general Hasdrubal has been killed, time contracts as one imagines other crowds gathering at street corners to hear the news of German and Japanese surrenders.

Livy shows that the vigor it takes to face our adversaries must ultimately come from pride in our own past and our achievements. Romanticizing our past is something to be cultivated, rather than to be ashamed of.

Livy offers other lessons, too. When after a military defeat Rome opts for a dictator, Livy explains that because "a sick body is more sensitive to the least pain than a healthy one," a despairing country will choose an extreme solution after only a minor reversal.[27] Peru's choice of the quasi-dictator Alberto Fujimori in 1990—and, more recently, Venezuela's of General Hugo Chavez and Pakistan's of General Pervez Musharraf—illustrate that truth. When Carthage breaks a nonaggression pact with Rome, Livy notes that "points of law" are largely meaningless unless they mirror the balance of power on the ground[28]—a point that the French humanist Raymond Aron also makes nineteen centuries later:

> Men know that in the long run international law must bow to fact. A territorial status invariably ends up being legalized, provided it lasts. A great power that wants to forbid a rival from making conquests must arm and not proclaim in advance a moral disapproval. . . .[29]

The scenes of frightful carnage—of men sleeping on corpses, of whole villages slaughtered, of battle so intense that even an earthquake is ignored—show in vivid detail that the horrors of war have not changed.[30] After reading Livy, one might even imagine Vietnam being remembered a hundred years hence as an obscure border conflict at the fringes of the American Cold War imperium, one that rent for a time the bond between the ruling elite and a large part of the citizenry. Or Vietnam might be seen as another Syracuse, the rich Sicilian city that the Athenians tried to subdue during the Peloponnesian War in an expedition that failed miserably because—as with our Vietnam policy in the early 1960s—unwise leaders tried to conquer too much, too far away.

Both the Second Punic War and World War II are episodes in an endless drama of momentous stakes, whose plot is never determined in advance and which we have the power to alter throughout, provided we believe in ourselves the way Rome did when challenged by Hannibal. Though Livy's history may detract from the uniqueness of our own struggles, it also shows just how heroic those struggles may seem millennia from now, when future generations will be inspired by our victories over fascism and communism the way Livy inspires us with his story of Rome's victory over Carthage. That is how Churchill thought of the ancient past, and this is how our leaders should think of it, too.

CHAPTER IV

SUN-TZU AND

THUCYDIDES

A foreign crisis, like war, "is the province of uncertainty . . . hidden in the fog of a greater or lesser uncertainty," according to the Prussian general Karl von Clausewitz. And in that fog of uncertainty, a wide-ranging intellect "is called for to feel out the truth with instinctive judgment."[1]

Foreign policy is the opposite of comprehensive knowledge: even with the best spies, area experts, and satellite surveillance, a critical area of darkness remains, caused not only by the absence of information but also by its surfeit, and the confusion it can lead to. Instinctive judgment is vital. A president or leader may be weak intellectually but can still show good judgment. Machiavelli, paraphrasing Cicero, explains that an ordinary man who values freedom will often recognize the truth.[2] Ronald Reagan was such a man.[3] Reagan, like Harry Truman, was better-read than most people think (Truman carried Plutarch with him on his travels), but both lacked intellectual pretensions and academic training and both were sneered at by the policy elites of their day.

A secretary of state or foreign minister must convert a president's impulses into a complex performance. That requires intellectual seasoning, of which literature is the great provider, because it augments one's own experience with the acumen of the finest minds. For example, Clausewitz, who defined war and strategy for nineteenth- and twentieth-century readers, steeped himself in the romantic plays and poetry of Friedrich von Schiller and the moral philosophy of Immanuel Kant.[4]

If literature is the quiet resource of statesmen, then no literature is more relevant for our purposes than the ancient classics on war and politics, which provide an emotional distance from the present that is especially valuable in a media age, when too many of us have become creatures of the moment—obsessed with the latest news event or opinion survey to the degree that it seems as if the past and all its lessons have ceased to exist.

The greater the disregard of history, the greater the delusions regarding the future. The expectation that a sprawling, multiethnic Russia, which had little exposure to the Enlightenment, would have a successful democratic transition comparable to that of small, uniethnic Poland—which was steeped in the traditions of Central Europe—showed a disregard of Russian history and geography; calls for a speedy transition to democracy in China overlook the violence and turmoil that occurred when previous Chinese dynasties collapsed, as well as the uneven record of democracy in places with weak institutions, a small or nonexistent middle class, and ethnic divides.

The classics help counter such historical amnesia. Machiavelli writes:

... anyone wishing to see what is to be must consider what has been: all the things of this world in every era have their counterparts in ancient times . . . since these actions are carried out by men who have and have always had the same passions, which, of necessity, must give rise to the same results.[5]

Confucius puts it more simply:

Being fond of the truth, I am an admirer of antiquity.[6]

To read the eminent thinkers of pagan antiquity is to find an unusual coherence, clarity of analysis, and unanimity of convictions, variously expressed. Because miscalculation in antiquity could result in painful execution, political philosophy had a pellucid edge. This is true not only of the sages of Greece and Rome, but of those of ancient China, too.

Mediterranean and Chinese civilizations emerged almost simultaneously, each unaware of the other for thousands of years—as if there were intelligent life existing elsewhere in the galaxy, going through tribulations vaguely similar to our own with both species destined to meet in some advanced technological era. In the late third century B.C., at the apex of the Roman Republic, when Rome and Carthage were fighting the First and Second Punic Wars, the Warring States of China merged under the Han overlordship. The Han ascendancy ended a process that saw strong Chinese states dominate weaker ones, only to be replaced by even stronger states. Despite periods of anarchy, feudalism was gradually giving way in China to an embryonic bureaucracy. In short, differences between Chinese and Mediterranean civilizations notwithstanding, the division of China's peoples into different groups and sovereignties led—as in the Mediterranean—to war, conquest, and power politics; so that the ancient philosophers of China, Greece, and Rome drew similar conclusions about human nature.

There is arguably no work of philosophy in which knowledge and experience are so pungently condensed as Sun-Tzu's *The Art of Warfare*. If Churchill's morality is summarized by his hardheadedness and Livy's by his patriotic virtue, then Sun-Tzu's morality is the warrior's honor—and the most honorable warrior is so great in the political sphere that military endeavors are avoided altogether.

Sun-Tzu's life is not grounded by a single historical fact.[7] Though he was likely a court minister in China in the fourth century B.C., it is also possible that he did not exist at all. *The Art of Warfare* may represent the accumulated wisdom of many people who experienced the chaotic period of the Warring States prior to the relative stability of Han rule in the late third century B.C. Whatever the truth, *The Art of Warfare* is not a military textbook so much as a work of philosophy by a writer who knows war firsthand and hates it, yet recognizes its unfortunate necessity on occasion.

The battles of the Warring States period involved archers, chariots, and foot soldiers who formed lines hundreds of miles long through mountains and swamps. Campaigns featured tens of thousands of men, both conscripts and professional warriors. The suffering was extraordinary. So if some of Sun-Tzu's advice, particularly what he says regarding spies, sounds extreme, it is because he knows from experience that extreme measures are often necessary to avert war without dishonoring oneself.

Sun-Tzu explains that in war the "highest excellence" is never having to fight, for the commencement of battle signifies a political failure. War, as Clausewitz would repeat 2,300 years after Sun-Tzu, is an unwanted yet sometimes necessary extension of politics. Sun-Tzu notes that the best way to avoid war—the violent result of political failure—is to think strategically. The strategic pursuit of self-interest is not a cold and amoral pseudo-science, but the moral act of those who know the horrors of battle and seek to avoid them.

A commander in chief who "plans and calculates like a hungry man" may avoid war, according to Sun-Tzu. Had President Bill Clinton, for example, concentrated on Kosovo with the same intensity in the months prior to the start of the spring 1999 NATO air war that he demonstrated during the war itself, he might have been able to avoid fighting in the first place. Had President George Bush concentrated more effectively on Iraq in the months prior to Saddam Hussein's August 1990 invasion of Kuwait, he too might not have needed to resort to war.

Agreeing with Confucius, Sun-Tzu asserts that a true commander is never swayed by public opinion, for virtue can be the opposite of fame or popularity.[8] (Plutarch, who considered "popularity" and "tyranny" the "same fault," insinuated that one led to the other.[9]) Sun-Tzu's example of a virtuous commander is one "who advances without any thought of winning personal fame and withdraws in spite of certain punishment" if it is in the interest of his army and people. In the 1920s, while reconstituting a Turkish state from the carcass of the Ottoman empire, Mustafa Kemal "Atatürk" frequently advanced his army against great odds, with considerable physical risk to himself. In the 1930s, he withdrew his claim from oil-rich territory in Iraq for the sake of regional stability, a gesture that Sun-Tzu would have applauded.

Sun-Tzu sanctions every manner of deceit, provided it is necessary to gain strategic advantage in order to avoid war. Because avoiding war requires forethought, he makes a strong case for spies:

> [F]oreknowledge cannot be had from ghosts and spirits. . . . It must come from people—people who know the enemy's situation. . . . Thus only those farsighted rulers and their superior commanders who can get the most intelligent people as their spies are destined to accomplish great things.[10]

Good spies prevent bloodshed, according to Sun-Tzu. A society like our own, which often heaps scorn on espionage and thus fails to attract its best people to the intelligence profession, is a society destined to stumble periodically into unnecessary wars. An irony of the post–World War II generation (and of the media, which reflects its values) is that it proclaims an era of human rights while abusing the profession that historically provides advance warning of gross human rights violations.

Sima Qian, the chronicler of the Qin and Han dynasties, who wrote in the first and second centuries B.C. (two hundred years after Sun-Tzu), also sanctions deceit to avoid bloodshed. "Great actions do not wait on petty scruples, abundant virtue does not trouble with niceties," he writes. "He who looks after the little and forgets the big will surely pay for it later."[11] Spies by necessity consort with sordid, immoral people. If you want to infiltrate Colombian drug gangs, you must have leeway to recruit thugs. Nice people will simply not be credible in such a criminal culture. Intelligence work involves years of toil, often at great personal risk, to achieve the slenderest result. Great successes go unreported to protect those involved. Intelligence gathering was a fundamental ingredient in the West's victory in the Cold War. If the media exposes a petty wrongdoing while ignoring the larger, unseen benefit of our national security agencies, they violate the dictums of both Sun-Tzu and Sima Qian.

Sun-Tzu and Sima Qian write as if they have experienced large-scale physical suffering firsthand, and they will go to almost any length to prevent its recurrence. Theirs is a morality of consequence that finds echoes in the ancient Greeks and Romans, as well as in Machiavelli and Churchill.

Chinese philosophy combines icy, morally detached observation with a moral response. Greek philosophy is similar.

Herodotus's account of the wars between Greece and Persia in the early fifth century B.C. is usually not judgmental. He "was dealing with the acts of men; and he looked upon them as fascinating revelations, as the naturalists had noted the planets and the stars, the seasons and the weather."[12] For Herodotus, who traveled widely through the Mediterranean and the Near East, men could have been mice in a cage. His detached inquisitiveness helps explain the alluring timelessness of his accounts.

Greece's victory over Persia, described by Herodotus, led, tragically, to a conflict between the Greek city-states themselves, known as the Peloponnesian War. That war was chronicled by Thucydides, who, born around 460 B.C., was a generation younger than Herodotus.

Thucydides was raised in a family of wealth and influence. His father owned extensive gold mines in Thrace, in northern Greece.

With estates and political connections in both Thrace and Athens, he was able to develop a comprehensive knowledge of Greece, and came into contact with the men who shaped the history of his time. Thucydides was in Athens in 430 B.C., at the outbreak of a plague that he too contracted. Having survived the disease, in 424 B.C. he was elected, along with another general, Eucles, to defend Thrace against Spartan forces. In November of that year, Eucles was in the Thracian city of Amphipolis when Spartan forces launched a surprise attack in a snowstorm. Thucydides' army was off the island of Thasos and could not return in time to save the city. The capture of Amphipolis sent shock waves through Athens. The blame evidently fell on Thucydides, whom the Athenians banished.

For the next two decades, Thucydides, now in disgrace, divided his time between his property in Thrace and his travels throughout the Spartan-dominated Peloponnesus. Thucydides' *Peloponnesian War* is the work not merely of a military historian, but of someone who has known firsthand disease, battle, and political humiliation, and encounters with both sides.

The Peloponnesian War may be the seminal work of international relations theory of all time. It is the first work to introduce a comprehensive pragmatism into political discourse. Its lessons have been elaborated upon by such writers as Hobbes, Hamilton, Clausewitz, and, in our own era, Hans Morgenthau, George F. Kennan, and Henry Kissinger. In contrast to Sun-Tzu and Cicero, whose works are rich in maxims, Thucydides is a military man, whose philosophy emerges naturally from his description of violent events. While Thucydides' persistent focus on self-interest may be offensive to some, his notion that self-interest gives birth to effort, and effort to options, makes his 2,400-year-old history of the Peloponnesian War a corrective to the extreme fatalism basic to Marxism and medieval Christianity.[13]

The war between Athens and Sparta, the subject of *The Peloponnesian War,* was not simply a clash between two city-states. Athens and Sparta each oversaw alliances of many smaller city-states, as complex and difficult to manage as either bloc in the Cold War. In Book Five—the story of "the peace that failed"—Thucydides demonstrates that decision making in antiquity required a mastery of variables no less numerous and complex than those faced by an American president.[14]

In 421 B.C., Athens and Sparta signed a peace treaty. Sparta wanted a respite from the war with Athens in order to put military pressure on Argos and its other neighbors in the Peloponnesus, the southern part of mainland Greece. But Sparta's allies in Thrace and Chalcidice (in northern Greece) refused to become subjects of Athens, which was one of the treaty's provisions. Back in the Peloponnesus, meanwhile, the great city-state of Corinth allied itself with Argos to prevent Sparta from dominating the region. In the central Peloponnesus, the city-state of Mantinea, which had recently conquered a number of smaller cities, joined Corinth and Argos to protect its new mini-empire against Sparta. Soon the Chalicidians also joined the anti-Sparta alliance. But Boeotia and Megara, both of which were threatened by democratic Athens, came to Sparta's aid. Sparta needed Boeotia's help to capture Panactum, a city close to Athens, which the Spartans hoped to trade with the Athenians for Pylos, in the Peloponnesus. As time went on, new men rose to power in Athens and Sparta who had not negotiated the peace treaty and, thus, were less committed to it. Ultimately, Sparta's treaty with Athens fell apart, and the two bipolar powers resumed their war.

If the above description seems utterly confusing, imagine trying to explain the intricacies of Cold War alliances to readers a few hundred years from now. Indeed, the slowness and difficulty of transportation in ancient Greece made it in relative terms as vast as the world. Thus, Thucydides' description of naked and labyrinthine calculations of power and interest is an apt metaphor for contemporary global politics.

Athens and Sparta came to blows because of uncontrollable allies: a reason that Russia, Germany, France, and Britain went to war in 1914. Had Churchill not saved the West from Hitler, World War I might now be seen as the beginning of the West's decline—much as the Peloponnesian War started the permanent decline of classical Greece.

Thucydides' military history leads him to the following conclusion:

Whatever we may think or profess, human behavior is guided by fear (*phobos*), self-interest (*kerdos*), and honor (*doxa*).[15] These aspects of human nature cause war and instability, accounting for *anthropinon,* the "human condition." The human condition, in turn, leads to political crises: when *physis* (pure instinct) triumphs over *nomoi* (laws), politics fails and is replaced by anarchy.[16] The solution to anarchy is not to deny fear, self-interest, and honor but to manage them for the sake of a moral outcome.

Thucydides' account of the conflict between Athens and the city of Mytilene—on the island of Lesbos, in the eastern Aegean Sea—is an example of his illusion-free insight into human behavior:

Mytilene had been an ally of Athens in the war against Persia.

The Mytileneans always feared the Athenians, but they feared Persia even more. It was self-interest, more than religion and patriotism, that inspired their alliance with Athens. In fact, without the war between Greece and Persia, which necessitated unity among the Greek city-states, there might not have been peace between Athens and Mytilene, or between Athens and Sparta. Thucydides notes that even after the war with Persia, Sparta refrained from violence against Athens out of respect for the latter's naval power. But once Athens's military position appeared to weaken, violence ensued. Thus, the concept of balance of power entered political thought with Thucydides.

In a plea for Spartan support against Athens, the Mytileneans appeal not to the ideals of the Spartans but to their self-interest. Their island holds a strategic position, the Mytileneans tell the Spartans—their navy is strong, and they can provide the Spartans with vital intelligence about the Athenians.

Thucydides' harshest example of how power and self-interest motivate our calculations is the so-called Melian Dialogue. Melos is a neutral island in the central Aegean, militarily vulnerable to Athens. The Athenians land a force on the island and arrogantly tell the Melians:

> . . . since you know as well as we do that right, as the world goes,
> is only in question between equals in power, while the strong do
> what they can and the weak suffer what they must.[17]

In other words, because Melos is weak, it can be treated unfairly. The Athenians have no strategic need for Melos, but they regard it as a prize owed to them for leading the Greek city-states against Persia. Thucydides suggests that the Athenians have no tragic sense of the future: they think that their greatness will last forever, and therefore believe that they can act with impunity. They are fearless, which can lead to arrogance. A completely amoral foreign policy, according to Thucydides, is neither practical nor prudent.

The Athenians never consider that the Melians will actually fight—an assumption that proves to be wrong. A protracted war erupts between Athens and Melos that ends when the Athenians— after the Melians have surrendered—slay the adult Melian males and enslave the women and children. Blinded by their high opinion of themselves, the dark victory of the Athenians over the Melians is a prelude to Athens's own military disaster in Sicily (similar to our own in Vietnam) less than three years later. Just as in Vietnam, the Athenians ignored signs of imminent danger even as they became more deeply involved:

> So thoroughly had the present prosperity persuaded the Athenians that nothing could withstand them, and that they could achieve what was possible and what was impracticable alike, with means ample or inadequate it mattered not. The reason for this was their general extraordinary success, which made them confuse their strength with their hopes.[18]

The Peloponnesian War teaches how power and affluence blinded Athens to the bleak forces of human nature that lie just beneath the veneer of civilization, threatening its good fortune. For example, early in the war, after hearing a funeral oration by the Athenian statesman Pericles that celebrates virtue, the Athenians' every-man-for-himself reaction to a disease outbreak exposes their *lack* thereof.

Thucydides' description of double-think and calculated atrocities shows that the totalitarian ills of the twentieth century are less unique than we might think.[19] For what shocks us about the Nazis is that their crimes occurred in a socially advanced, industrialized society, where atavistic instincts were thought to have been vanquished. Yet it is precisely the taboos imposed by civilization that can make hatred feel at times like a "renewal of virility."[20] Thucydides teaches us that civilization represses barbarism but can never eradicate it.[21] Thus, the more socially and economically advanced the times, the more necessary it is for leaders to maintain a sense of their societies' fallibility and vulnerability: that is the ultimate defense against catastrophe.

Central to the philosophy of Thucydides and Sun-Tzu is the idea that war is not an aberration. Elaborating upon the ancient Greeks and Chinese, the mid-twentieth-century French philosopher Raymond Aron and his Spanish contemporary José Ortega y Gasset both observe that war is inherent in the division of humanity into states and other groupings.[22] Sovereignty and alliances rarely occur in a void; they arise from differences with others. The counterpart to war in Chinese, *an,* though conventionally translated as "peace," really means "stability."[23] Thus, as Aron notes, while our ideals have usually been peaceful, history has often been violent.[24] Though this should be obvious, it bears repeating given the triumphalist tone of public discourse in the aftermath of the Cold War. Somehow the collapse of an overly centralized Soviet state and the withdrawal of the Red Army from Central Europe, rather than being seen as a return to a more normal pattern of conflict, has been greeted as evidence that civil society is on the horizon across the globe.

Because humanity, as Thucydides shows, is divided into groups that are in incessant competition with each other, the central characteristic of all states is their maneuverability: rarely can states be categorized as strictly good or evil. Instead, they tend to act good for a while and bad for a while, or good on one issue and bad on another, as they endlessly navigate for advantage. That is why the term "rogue state," though occasionally appropriate, may also expose the idealistic illusions of its user: since it misjudges the nature of states themselves.

Recognizing that good and evil are usually false dichotomies for states, Raymond Aron writes (again, echoing Thucydides and Sun-Tzu) that criticism of idealism "is not only pragmatic, it is also moral," because "idealistic diplomacy slips too often into fanaticism. . . ."[25] Indeed, the acceptance of a world governed by a pagan notion of self-interest exemplified by Thucydides makes statesmanship likelier to succeed: it curtails illusions, reducing the scope for miscalculation. Historically grounded liberalism recognizes that liberty did not arise from abstract reflection, moral or otherwise, but from difficult political choices made by rulers acting in their own self-interest. As the Danish classicist and historian David Gress notes, liberty grew in the West mainly because it served the interest of power.[26]

CHAPTER V

MACHIAVELLIAN VIRTUE

Machiavelli was a popularizer of ancient thinking, though he often disagreed with its particulars and gave it his own original and radical twist. Machiavelli believed that because Christianity glorified the meek, it allowed the world to be dominated by the wicked: he preferred a pagan ethic that elevated self-preservation over the Christian ethic of sacrifice, which he considered hypocritical.[1] Nevertheless, one must be careful with Machiavelli. Because he often reduces politics to mere technique and cunning, it is easy to find justification in his writing for almost any policy.

The late-twentieth-century Middle East shows Machiavelli's piercing insight into human behavior:

In 1988, during the Palestinian Intifada, Israel's defense minister, Yitzhak Rabin, reportedly told Israeli soldiers to "go in and break their bones," referring to Palestinian protesters. Less violent means had failed to quell the demonstrators, while the use of live bullets resulted in Palestinian casualties that ignited further riots.

The outside world was pressuring Israel to compromise with the Palestinians. Instead, Rabin chose to "break their bones." He knew that only enfeebled, poorly led regimes, like that of the late Shah of Iran, compromise with street anarchy. Rabin's actions were condemned by American liberals. But Rabin's standing in Israeli opinion polls began suddenly to rise. In 1992, hard-line Israeli voters switched to the dovish Labor party only because Rabin headed the ticket. Once elected prime minister, Rabin used his new power to make peace with the Palestinians and Jordanians. Rabin, assassinated by a right-wing extremist in 1995, is now a hero for liberal humanists the world over.

Rabin's Western admirers prefer to forget his ruthlessness against the Palestinians, but Machiavelli would have understood that such tactics were central to Rabin's "virtue." In an imperfect world, Machiavelli says, good men bent on doing good must know how to be bad. And because we all share the social world, he adds, virtue has little to do with individual perfection and everything to do with political result. Thus, for Machiavelli, a policy is defined not by its excellence but by its outcome: if it isn't effective, it can't be virtuous.[2]

Like Machiavelli, Churchill, Sun-Tzu, and Thucydides all believed in a morality of results rather than of good intentions. So did Raymond Aron. After Hitler came to power, seeing that France's policy of disarmament and negotiation with Germany were no substitute for military preparedness, Aron wrote, "A good policy is measured by its effectiveness," not by its purity— testimony to the fact that Machiavelli's self-evident truths are independently rediscovered in every age.[3]

Rabin's tough tactics gave him the credibility to make peace;

thus, his tactics displayed Machiavellian virtue. Rabin was only as brutal as the circumstances required, and no more. Then he turned his reputation for brutality to the benefit of his fellow citizens— something also recommended by Machiavelli. Rabin did not relent simply to avoid a reputation for violence while allowing disorder to continue. Here, too, he acted like a true *prince*.

By contrast, the decision of the Clinton administration in its first term to make the renewal of China's most-favored-nations trade status dependent solely on an improvement in China's human rights record was not virtuous—not because the policy failed to achieve an improvement in human rights in China, but because it was clear from the start that it would fail.[4] The policy was sanctimonious, undertaken with little hope of practical results, merely to demonstrate what the administration assumed was its superior morality.

In 1999, the United Nations sanctioned a referendum on independence in the Indonesian-held island of East Timor that sparked well-organized attacks by anti-independence militias, in which the capital, Dili, was burned and thousands murdered—in many cases tortured and decapitated. This terror rampage was easily foreseen. For months beforehand, the United Nations had been repeatedly told what would happen if it held elections without security guarantees.[5] Thus, in its startling lack of foresight, weak planning, and chaotic implementation, the U.N.'s exercise in democracy lacked Machiavellian virtue.

In 1957, King Hussein of Jordan dissolved a democratically elected government that was becoming increasingly radical and pro-Soviet, and imposed martial law. Then, in 1970, and again in the 1980s, he cracked down brutally on the Palestinians, who had tried violently to topple his regime. Yet King Hussein's antidemocratic acts saved his kingdom from forces that would have been crueler than himself. Like his "brother in peace," Rabin, the Jordanian monarch employed only so much violence and no more. His violence, therefore, was central to his "virtue."

The Chilean dictator Augusto Pinochet, on the other hand, employed excessive violence and thus lacks Machiavellian virtue. Machiavelli would have frowned upon Pinochet, the United Nations in East Timor, and Clinton's initial policy toward China; but he might have lifted a glass in honor of Rabin and King Hussein in the quiet of his Tuscan farmhouse, and smiled.

By substituting pagan for Christian virtue, Machiavelli has explained better than any contemporary expert how Rabin and Hussein became what they were. Nor is there anything amoral about Machiavelli's pagan virtue. Isaiah Berlin writes: "Machiavelli's values are not Christian, but they are moral values"—the Periclean and Aristotelian values of the ancient *polis;* the values that secure a stable political community.[6]

Thucydides writes about virtue and so do many Roman writers, particularly Sallust.[7] But Machiavelli elaborates on it. "Virtue," or *virtù,* in Machiavelli's Italian, derives ultimately from *vir,* Latin for "man." For Machiavelli, virtue variously means "valor," "ability," "ingenuity," "determination," "energy," and "prowess": manly vigor, that is, but usually in the pursuit of the general good.[8] Virtue presupposes ambition, but not only for the sake of personal advancement.

In Chapter 8 of *The Prince,* Machiavelli cites Agathocles the Sicilian, who became ruler of Syracuse in the late fourth century B.C., noting that "luck or favour played little or no part" in Agathocles' success. Rather, it was "through overcoming countless difficulties and dangers" that he "rose up through the ranks of the militia, and gained power." Nonetheless, Machiavelli says, "it cannot be called virtue to kill one's fellow-citizens, to betray one's friends, to be treacherous, merciless and irreligious" for no higher purpose, as was the case with Agathocles.

Machiavelli's pagan virtue is public virtue, whereas Judeo-Christian virtue is more often private virtue. A famous example of good public virtue and bad private virtue might be President Franklin Delano Roosevelt's somewhat mischievous evasions of truth in getting an isolationist Congress to approve the Lend-Lease Act in 1941, which allowed for the transfer of war supplies to England. "In effect," writes the playwright Arthur Miller about Roosevelt, "mankind is in debt to his lies."[9] In his *Discourses on Livy,* Machiavelli sanctions fraud when it is necessary for the well-being of the *polis.*[10] This is not a new or cynical idea: Sun-Tzu writes that politics and war constitute "the art of deceit," which, if practiced wisely, may lead to victory and the reduction of casualties.[11] That this is a dangerous precept and easily misused does not strip it of positive applications.

Of course, the military virtue of Machiavelli and Sun-Tzu is not always appropriate to civil leadership. Generals should use deceit; judges should not. I am talking only about foreign policy, in which violence and the threat of it are employed without recourse to any court. Though international institutions are strengthening, they are not nearly developed enough to change this brutal fact.

Niccolò Machiavelli was born in 1469 in Florence to an impoverished member of a noble family. His father could not afford to give him a good education, and Machiavelli labored under obscure teachers. To some extent, he was self-taught, which saved him from the scholastic abstractions that tainted the culture of his age. Machiavelli's opportunity came in 1498, with the execution of Girolamo Savonarola, an austere monk whose extreme politics led to a popular backlash and the election of a more moderate republican government in the city-state of Florence. Machiavelli, then twenty-nine, became secretary to the republic's military and diplomatic council. For the next fourteen years he was one of Florence's leading diplomats, traveling in the France of Louis XII and gaining exposure to civilizations different from his own. When the collapse of the Borgia dynasty threw central Italy into confusion, Machiavelli, in 1505, visited the leading oligarchs of Perugia and Siena in an attempt to make them allies of Florence. The next year, he observed firsthand the fiery subjugation of Perugia and Emilia by the warrior pope Julius II. While sending dispatches to Florence on the progress of Julius's campaign, Machiavelli had to visit the camps of Florentine soldiers, paying their levies in the struggle to retake Pisa. Yet as soon as Pisa was recovered in 1509, Florence found itself threatened by both France and Spain.

Machiavelli's political career ended abruptly in 1512 with the invasion of Italy by Spanish forces loyal to Pope Julius. Faced with the sacking of their city, the Florentines surrendered, and their republic—with its civic institutions—was dissolved. A progressive by nature, Machiavelli had replaced the republic's mercenary forces with citizens' militias. But the new militias failed to save Florence, and the Medici family returned from exile as the ruling oligarchs. Machiavelli immediately made overtures to them, but in vain: the Medicis dismissed him from his post, then accused him of taking part in a conspiracy against the new regime.

After being imprisoned and tortured on the rack, Machiavelli was allowed to retire to his farm. It was there, in 1513, that he retreated every evening to his study and reflected on the history of ancient Greece and Rome, comparing it with his own considerable government experience, which, like Thucydides', included military responsibilities, failure, and public humiliation. The wisdom of both men was a consequence of their mistakes, bad fortune, and suffering. For Machiavelli, the result was *The Prince*, his most famous work on politics, published in 1532, after his death. It was a guide to help both Italy and his beloved Florence survive against intolerant foreign antagonists. In showing the reinstated Medici family how to bring honor upon themselves and Florence, Machiavelli wrote out of deep sadness for the human condition that he knew firsthand:

> I laugh, and my laughter is not within me;
> I burn, and the burning is not seen outside.[12]

The Italy that Machiavelli confronted was one divided into towns and city-states, "subject to death-dealing factions, *coups d'état,* assassinations, aggression, and defeat in war."[13] Machiavelli believed that "since one must start from the present state of things, one can only work with the material at hand."[14] Nevertheless, early-Renaissance Italy, as the artistic, literary, and economic record shows, had a deeply rooted civic culture helped by broad cultural commonalities. The anarchic situation common to Côte d'Ivoire, Nigeria, Pakistan, Indonesia, and other places today may actually be worse, so American policymakers, rather than stand on ceremony and condemn outright autocratic elements, will truly have no choice but to work with *the material at hand.* In Indonesia, for example, forcing the new democratic rulers to further alienate the military—before even consolidating their own power and institutions—would more likely lead to the bloody collapse of the country than to speedier democratization.

Machiavelli came up in the conversations I had with political and military leaders in Uganda and Sudan in the mid-1980s, in Sierra Leone in the early 1990s, and in Pakistan in the mid-1990s. In all of these places—threatened by corruption, anarchy, and ethnic violence—the challenge was to maintain civil order and the integrity of the state by whatever means available, with whatever allies were available. While the ultimate goal was moral, the means were sometimes offensive. In the cases of Uganda and Pakistan, it meant coups d'état. After General Pervez Musharraf overthrew the elected leader of Pakistan, Nawaz Sharif, in October 1999, Musharraf telephoned the commander in chief for U.S. forces in the Near East, General Anthony C. Zinni, and explained his actions in words that Machiavelli might well have used.

Defending Machiavelli, the scholar Jacques Barzun says that if he was indeed a "moral monster," then "a long list of thinkers"— including Aristotle, Saint Augustine, Saint Thomas, John Adams, Montesquieu, Francis Bacon, Spinoza, Coleridge, and Shelley—all of whom "have advised, approved, or borrowed Machiavellian maxims"—would "form a legion of fellow immoralists."[15] Yet suspicion of Machiavelli has turned his name into a synonym for cynicism and unscrupulousness. It is a hatred fanned originally by the Catholic Counter-Reformation, whose pieties Machiavelli exposed as masks for self-interest. Machiavelli, pre-eminent among Renaissance humanists, put his emphasis on men rather than on God.

Machiavelli's stress on political necessity rather than on moral perfection framed his philosophical attack on the Church. Thus, he left the Middle Ages and helped, along with others, inspire the Renaissance by renewing the link with Thucydides, Livy, Cicero, Seneca, and other classical thinkers of the West.[16] Machiavelli also takes up the same themes as the writers of ancient China. Both Sun-Tzu and the writers of the *Chan-kuo Ts'e*— the discourses of the Warring States period in China—believed, like Machiavelli, that men are naturally wicked and require moral training to be good. Also like Machiavelli, they emphasize the power of individual self-interest to shape and improve the world.

The Prince, as well as Machiavelli's *Discourses on Livy*, are full of bracing insight. Machiavelli writes that foreign invaders will support local minorities over the majority in order "to weaken those who are powerful within the country itself"—which is how European governments behaved in the Middle East in the nineteenth and early-twentieth centuries, when they armed ethnic minorities against the Ottoman rulers. He writes about the difficulty in toppling existing regimes because rulers, no matter how cruel, are surrounded by loyalists, who will suffer if the ruler is deposed; in this, he anticipated the difficulty of replacing dictators such as Saddam Hussein. "All armed prophets succeed whereas unarmed ones fail," he writes, anticipating the danger of a bin Laden. Savonarola was an unarmed prophet who failed, while the medieval popes, along with Moses and Mohammed, were armed prophets who triumphed. Hitler was an armed prophet, and it required an extraordinary effort to vanquish him. Only when Mikhail Gorbachev made it clear that he would not defend Communist regimes in Eastern Europe with force was it possible for the unarmed prophet Václav Havel to succeed.

Nevertheless, Machiavelli may go too far. Wasn't he himself an unarmed prophet who succeeded in influencing statesmen for centuries with only a book? Wasn't Jesus an unarmed prophet whose followers helped bring down the Roman empire? One must always keep in mind that ideas do matter, for better and worse, and to reduce the world merely to power struggles is to make cynical use of Machiavelli. But some academics and intellectuals go too far in the other direction: they try to reduce the world only to ideas, and to neglect power.

Values—good or bad—Machiavelli says, are useless without arms to back them up: even a civil society requires police and a credible judiciary to enforce its laws. Therefore, for policymakers, projecting power comes first; values come second. "The power to hurt is bargaining power. To exploit it is diplomacy," writes the political scientist Thomas Schelling.[17] Abraham Lincoln, the ultimate prince, understood this when he said that American geography was suited for one nation, not two, and that his side would prevail, provided it was willing to pay the cost in blood.[18] Machiavelli's prince, Cesare Borgia, failed to unite Italy against Pope Julius, but Lincoln was sufficiently ruthless to target the farms, homes, and factories of Southern civilians in the latter phase of the Civil War.[19] Thus Lincoln reunited the temperate zone of North America, preventing it from falling prey to European powers and creating a mass society under uniform laws.

Virtue is more complex than it seems. Because human rights are a self-evident good, we believe that by promoting them we are being virtuous. But that is not always the case. If the United States had pressed too hard for human rights in Jordan, King Hussein might have been weakened during his struggles for survival in the 1970s and 1980s. The same is true in Egypt, where a U.S. policy dominated completely by human rights concerns would weaken President Hosni Mubarak, whose successor would likely have even less regard for human rights. The same is true for Tunisia, Morocco, Turkey, Pakistan, the Republic of Georgia, and many other countries. Though regimes such as Azerbaijan, Uzbekistan, and China are oppressive, the power vacuum that would likely replace them would cause even more suffering.

For Machiavelli, virtue is the opposite of righteousness. With their incessant harping on values, today's Republicans and Democrats alike often sound less like Renaissance pragmatists than like medieval churchmen, dividing the world sanctimoniously between good and evil.

Isaiah Berlin's observation that Machiavelli's values are moral but not Christian raises the possibility of several just but incompatible value systems existing side by side. For example, had Lee Kuan Yew of Singapore subscribed to America's doctrine of individual liberties, the meritocracy, public honesty, and economic success fostered by his mild authoritarianism might have been impossible. While Singapore ranks near the top of key indexes on economic freedom—freedom from property confiscation, from capricious tax codes, from burdensome regulations, and so on— the West African state of Benin, a parliamentary democracy, stands in the bottom quarter of such indexes.[20]

Machiavelli's ideal is the "well-governed *patria*," not individual freedom. The "well-governed *patria*" may at times be incompatible with an aggressive media, whose search for the "truth" can yield little more than embarrassing facts untempered by context, so the risk of exposure may convince leaders to devise new methods of secrecy. The more the barons of punditry demand "morality" in complex situations overseas, where all the options are either bad or involve great risk, the more *virtù* our leaders may need in order to deceive them. Just as the priests of ancient Egypt, the rhetoricians of Greece and Rome, and the theologians of medieval Europe undermined political authority, so too do the media. While suspicion of power has been central to the American Creed, presidents and military commanders will have to regain breathing space from media assaults to deal with the challenges of split-second decision making in future warfare.

Machiavelli's ideals influenced the Founding Fathers of the United States. The Founders certainly had more faith in ordinary people than Machiavelli did. Nevertheless, their recollection of the debacle of Oliver Cromwell's parliamentary rule in mid-seventeenth-century England made them healthily suspicious of the masses. "Men are ambitious, vindictive, and rapacious," writes Alexander Hamilton, echoing Machiavelli (and, unwittingly, the ancient Chinese).²¹ That is why James Madison preferred a "republic" (in which the whims of the masses are filtered through "their representatives and agents") over direct "democracy," in which the people "exercise the government in person...."²²

The core of Machiavelli's wisdom is that primitive necessity and self-interest drive politics, and that this can be good in itself, because competing self-interests are the basis for compromise, while stiff moral arguments lead to war and civil conflict, rarely the better options.

Machiavelli emphasizes that "all the things of men are in motion and cannot remain fixed." Thus, primitive necessity is irresistible, because, as Harvard professor Harvey C. Mansfield explains, "A man or a country may be able to afford generosity today but what of tomorrow?"[23] The United States may have the power to intervene in East Timor today, but then can we afford to fight in the Taiwan Strait and the Korean Peninsula tomorrow? The answer may well be yes. If we have the means to stop a large-scale human rights tragedy, it is a good in and of itself to do so—provided that we confront our capabilities not only for this day, but for the next. In an age of constant crises, "anxious foresight" must be the centerpiece of any prudent policy.[24]

CHAPTER VI

FATE AND INTERVENTION

Machiavelli's notion of anxious foresight leads us to one of the most vexing questions of international relations: when does a war, atrocity, or other danger become foreseeable?

Polybius, writing in the second century B.C., believed that the origins of Alexander the Great's war against Persia in 333 B.C. lay decades earlier, in the lifetime of Alexander's father, Philip II. With his own career as a Greek statesman providing ample material to draw from, Polybius explained that "the cause comes first in a given chain of events and the beginning last."[1] By "the cause," he means the conditions "which influence in advance our purposes and decisions." By "the beginning," he means only the immediate actions that ignite a cataclysm.

Thus, the decisions taken by Yugoslav leaders in the late 1980s and early 1990s were merely "the beginning" of the recent war, not its cause. The cause might have originated in the Yugoslav civil war fought during World War II, or, more likely, in the early 1980s, when a crumbling economy, a decaying Cold War security structure, and an ethnic-Albanian insurrection against the Serbs in Kosovo combined to intensify ethnic strife and create conditions favorable to greater violence.

Conditions favorable does not signify inevitability, only a strong possibility if policymakers ignore the evidence. Yugoslavia was not so intractable or complex that Margaret Thatcher could not have stopped the war from spreading into Bosnia with the angry rap of her handbag at any of several NATO meetings in 1991 or early 1992, had she still been the British prime minister.

Since early warning is a sine qua non of crisis prevention, and because individual circumstances such as the Conservative party coup that toppled Thatcher from power in 1990 cannot be foreseen, foreign policy must be the art of intelligently organizing what information can be foreseen, so as to provide a framework, albeit indistinct, for future events—that is the lesson of Machiavelli's "anxious foresight."

What can be foreseen is what changes slowly or not at all: climate, the resource base, the pace of urbanization, interethnic relations, the strength of the middle class, and so on. One reason the United Nations keeps track of literacy and fertility rates (and then ranks countries in a "Human Development Index" according to such factors) is that they are descriptive of the present and instructive of the future.

The canceled second round of Algerian elections in January 1992 was not the cause of Algeria's Islamic terrorism and civil conflict but merely its "beginning." The causes include the astoundingly high rates of population increase and urbanization for decades prior to 1992, so hordes of frustrated, unemployed young males overwhelmed the cities and shantytowns.[2] There was also the reinvention of Islam in a modern and impersonal urban setting, giving it an ideological severity it lacked in the villages. These circumstances could easily have alerted policymakers to Algeria's increasing tendency for conflict.

In 1989, when the Berlin Wall fell, an analyst relying solely on the evidence of history, culture, and geography could have anticipated the condition of former Warsaw Pact countries a decade later. Before World War II and the Red Army flattened Eastern Europe, the Protestant-Catholic lands of eastern Germany, Poland, Hungary, and western Czechoslovakia—all once part of the advanced Habsburg empire—had boasted large and vibrant middle classes. Industrial production in western Czechoslovakia rivaled that of England and Belgium. Not so in the Eastern Orthodox Balkan nations and Russia, burdened by centuries of Byzantine, Ottoman, and czarist absolutism, where middle classes were tiny specks amid vast peasant populations. Of those poorer nations, Russia was always the worst off, its social fabric rent by more decades of communism than the Balkans, and its problems further complicated by sheer size, ethnic diversity, and proximity to the least stable parts of Asia. Not surprisingly, by 2000, the order of economic development in Eastern Europe was roughly what it had been prior to World War II, with the northern, ex-Habsburg part of the region the most prosperous, the Balkans further behind, and Russia in the worst condition. Croatia, meanwhile, befitting the destiny of a marchland between Central Europe and the Balkans, was torn by Balkan violence in the 1990s, but is now moving toward civil society faster than its southern neighbors.

There are exceptions to this historical and cultural pattern: Serbs, who are worse off than many urban Russians; ethnic-Hungarian Catholics in northern Serbia, who are worse off than Orthodox Romanians in Bucharest; and, most dramatically, Greece—an Eastern Orthodox, Balkan nation that ranks ahead of Poland, the Czech Republic, and Hungary on the United Nations Human Development Index.[3] But Greece's escape from communism and Balkan underdevelopment required an American-backed counterinsurgency against communist guerrillas, followed by $10 billion in Truman Doctrine aid (in 1940s dollars) for a country of only 7.5 million people, and gross interference by the Central Intelligence Agency in Greece's domestic politics through the 1950s.

The benefits of using historical and cultural models to glimpse the future are obvious, but so are the drawbacks. What if the Truman administration had abandoned Greece? In the late 1940s, Eastern Orthodox Greece was economically backward, without a traditional middle class, torn by civil strife, unexposed to the Western Enlightenment, and geographically and spiritually closer to Russia than to the West. History and geography clearly suggested that helping Greece was a lost cause. Yet, it succeeded. And as expensive as U.S. intervention in Greece turned out to be, it was cheap compared to the cost in American defense outlays and human suffering had Greece become a Soviet satellite in 1949.

The collapse of the Soviet Union is another argument against what Isaiah Berlin dismissed as "historical inevitability."[4] No matter how infirm the Soviet system was, the spectacle of a continental empire crumbling quickly on its own, with no invading army to instigate it, had few precedents in history. It was this dramatic, unforeseen conclusion to the Cold War that led one of Berlin's colleagues to declare: " 'Inevitability' has rather a bad track record."[5]

A stirring argument against inevitability is the *Shi ji,* or *Records of the Grand Historian,* by Sima Qian, the Thucydides of ancient China, whose history of the Qin and Han dynasties includes many passages like this:

> Chen She, born in a humble hut with tiny windows and a wattle door, a day labourer in the fields and a garrison conscript, whose abilities could not match even the average . . . led a band of several hundred poor, weary soldiers in a revolt against Qin. . . . The weapons which he improvised from hoes and tree branches could not match the sharpness of spears and battle pikes; his little band of garrison conscripts was nothing beside the armies of the Nine States. . . . Qin [was] a great kingdom and for 100 years made the ancient eight provinces pay homage at its court. Yet, after it had become master of the six directions . . . a single commoner [Chen She] opposed it and its seven ancestral temples toppled. . . .[6]

If the future were really discernible, political science would enjoy more respect than it does, and determinism—the belief that historical, cultural, economic, and other antecedent forces *determine* the future of both individuals and nations—would not be such a disreputable word. Wars have seldom been won by fatalism, and battlefield victories against great odds have regularly changed the direction of history. "One of the perennial infirmities of human beings," writes the late British historian Arnold Toynbee, "is to ascribe their own failure to forces that are entirely beyond their control."[7] A great leader needs some sense of idealism and possibility. Machiavelli's *Prince* has endured partly because it is an instructional guide for those who do not accept fate and require the utmost cunning to vanquish more powerful forces.

Yet, it hardly follows that policymakers should ignore all factors, objective and subjective, that forewarn them of crises, and which may prevent them.

Determinism has been argued about since the Greek Stoics identified two seemingly contradictory notions: individual moral responsibility and "causation"—the belief that our acts are the unavoidable result of a chain of prior events.[8] It was the determinism of the medieval Catholic Church, which believed that history had a single direction and purpose, that Machiavelli revolted against. Twentieth-century history makes determinism the pithiest philosophical issue facing policymakers today, for behind the errors of Marxism and other follies lay the error of reading from the past too narrowly into the future.

While Marxism is the classic case of a determinist philosophy, determinism was also a factor in the appeasement of Nazi Germany in the 1930s. Appeasement revealed the danger of a narrow fixation on power—who has it and who doesn't—which puts one in the awkward position of seizing it oneself or knuckling under. To wit, the pro-appeasement editor of *The Times* of London, Geoffrey Dawson, asked, "If the Germans are as powerful as" people say, "oughtn't we to go with them?"[9] Chamberlain believed Hitler's rearmament was a troubling but inevitable outcome of Germany's industrial capacity, its large and dynamic population, and its strategic position at the heart of Europe. Thus, the Nazi leader could not be stopped.

Unlike the respectable and upright Chamberlain, Churchill was a drinker and surrounded himself with a "disreputable crowd of *roués*."[10] It was precisely such a personality, unstable and overbearing, that was an antidote to Chamberlain's fatalism. Churchill's exuberance and sentimentality regarding the British empire made it impossible for him to imagine an outcome that the British prime minister did not help shape. Thus, he grasped the illogic of Chamberlain's attitude toward Hitler, which nullified the influence of Chamberlain himself.

Churchill was by nature a pluralist: someone who believes that many things (particularly his own actions) interact, and that no one thing *determines* the future. Like Ronald Reagan, another leader who proved more clairvoyant than the foreign affairs mandarinate that disdained him, Churchill was blessed with a moral passion—a "clean hatred"—that proved more effective than Chamberlain's pragmatism and fatalism.[11] Reagan's first inaugural address might have been lifted from Churchill: "I do not believe in a fate that will fall on us no matter what we do. I do believe in a fate that will fall on us if we do nothing."

It may have seemed irrational for Reagan to believe in the 1980s that the Cold War was temporary and that the Berlin Wall would collapse. Reagan thereby exposed another characteristic of determinism: that of being overly rational, a flaw to which policy analysts and other experts are especially prone. A merely rational man might not have challenged Hitler the way Churchill did.

Whereas Churchill and Reagan represented strategic and moral decisiveness against considerable odds, in 1993 President Clinton appeared to represent the fatalism of the appeasers by failing to intervene in the former Yugoslavia to stop war crimes committed by Bosnian Serbs against Bosnian Moslems.

Some of the strongest criticism against Clinton's failure to intervene early in Bosnia came from the admirers of Isaiah Berlin, whose defense of the right of the individual to act against gross injustice and the constraints of history, culture, and geography hovered in the background throughout the Bosnia debate. Both Berlin and Churchill abhorred determinism, yet Churchill's geographical and cultural portrait of Sudan in *The River War* is full of it. Explaining this apparent contradiction is necessary in order to differentiate anxious foresight, which is sensible, from determinism, which often is not.

At the height of the Cold War, when the social sciences were ascendant, with their promise of solutions if only enough data on human behavior could be assembled—a time when many scholars spurned bourgeois values for Marxist utopias and proclaimed all men "political animals"—Isaiah Berlin, who lived in and taught at Oxford, defended bourgeois pragmatism, supported "temporizing compromises" over political experimentation, doubted the values of the social sciences, and was skeptical of the benefits of political participation.[12] He personifies the skepticism and intellectual courage to which all statesmen should aspire.

Berlin's attack on determinism was summed up in a lecture he delivered in 1953 and published the following year, under the title "Historical Inevitability," in which he condemns as immoral and cowardly the belief that *vast impersonal forces* such as biology, geography, the environment, the laws of economics, and ethnic characteristics determine our lives.[13] Berlin reproaches Toynbee and Edward Gibbon for seeing "nations" and "civilizations" as "more 'concrete' " than the individuals who embody them, and for seeing abstractions like "Tradition" and "History" as "wiser than we." Michael Ignatieff, Berlin's biographer, writes:

> [T]he core of his moral outlook lay in a fierce dislike of attempts to deny human beings their right to moral sovereignty. Communism and fascism alike were guilty of this in the very way they sought to indoctrinate their adherents and liquidate their enemies.[14]

Geography, group characteristics, and so on influence but do not *determine* our lives; individuals are more concrete than the nations to which they belong; free thought is central to our nature; and while History may somehow be wiser than we, we cannot know its direction, even though policymakers must use all the means at their disposal to anticipate events. While these points seem self-evident, it took courage to assert them in the academic world that Berlin inhabited, which was then in the throes of Marxism and other social science fads.

Today the Marxism and fascism against which Berlin directs his attacks have been vanquished. But other deterministic ideologies— radical Islam and blind faith in technology, for instance—will continue to evolve, which is why I believe that Berlin's antitotalitarian literature will long survive the twentieth century. Nevertheless, today's foreign policy challenges cannot be solved without some reference to the environment, demographics, historical circumstances, and other factors that Berlin, in his sweeping attacks on all forms of determinism, seems at first glance to reject.

Paraphrasing the German philosopher Immanuel Kant, Berlin says that determinism is incompatible with morality because only those "who are the true authors of their own acts . . . can be praised or blamed for what they do."[15] He is not saying that the environment, demographics, and historical circumstances do not matter, or that they do not affect individual choice: only that in the final analysis every one of us—journalists, statesmen, ethnic warlords, and so on—must take moral responsibility for our actions, however much they may be influenced by outside forces. Recognizing how the environment influences actions and desires, Berlin writes:

> Men who live in conditions where there is not sufficient food, warmth, shelter, and the minimum degree of security can scarcely be expected to concern themselves with freedom of contract or of the press.[16]

Forecasting on the basis of fertility and urbanization rates emphasizes group behavior over personal choice and rests fundamentally on an assumption of biological determinism: the reaction of primates to the stress of overcrowding. This is true, for instance, of forecasts of mass violence in Rwanda before 1994 based on diminishing soil fertility, soaring population growth (the average Rwandan woman conceived eight times over her life span), and the record of large-scale ethnic killing in the 1960s and 1970s.[17] Forecasting violence did not make it inevitable and might even have helped prevent it, had officials taken the predictions seriously enough and acted in time.

This may seem like belaboring the obvious, yet there has been a tendency among some journalists and intellectuals to label such forecasts as deterministic merely because they warn of bleak consequences.

The Center for Army Analysis in Washington, which has compiled an impressive record of anticipating instability in various regions, rates countries almost as actuaries do people: individual moral choice plays little or no part in its analyses, while *vast impersonal forces* like demography and history play a great role. The Center's methods are not unique in the American military and intelligence community. Relying in large measure on historical trends, especially a tendency for ethnic strife, the Central Intelligence Agency warned in a national intelligence estimate of the violent breakup of Yugoslavia a year before it happened. This was a legitimate assumption in the service of anxious foresight. When Berlin castigates determinism, he never says that we should ignore imminent signs of danger.

Thus, when Churchill wrote about the effect of geography, climate, and history on the African and Arab inhabitants of Sudan, he was not being fatalistic; he was only reporting what he knew and had experienced, thereby showing what an extraordinary effort would be required to change things there.

Such candor is absolutely necessary. To treat every country and crisis as a clean slate full of hopeful possibilities is dangerous; what is achievable in one place may not be in another. In that vein, Raymond Aron writes of a "sober ethic rooted in the truth of 'probabilistic determinism,' " because "human choice always operates within certain contours or restraints such as the inheritance of the past. . . ."[18] The key word here is "probabilistic," that is, a partial or hesitant determinism which recognizes obvious differences between groups and regions but does not oversimplify, and leaves many possibilities open. Bold statesmanship never makes foolhardy bets based on hope; it works near the edges of what seems attainable in a given situation, for even the most dire situations can have better and worse outcomes.

Thus, a responsible foreign policy requires a limited degree of determinism. It also requires a limited amount of appeasement: never to capitulate to gross human rights violations might mean having U.S. troops patrolling not only in Somalia, Haiti, Bosnia, and Kosovo, but also in Abkhazia, Nagorno-Karabakh, Kashmir, Rwanda, Burundi, northeastern Congo, Sierra Leone, Liberia, Angola, and many other places. The creation of a global constabulary force—organized by the United States and other powers under U.N. auspices—would make frequent interventions more practical. Yet there would still be arguments on where to intervene, especially if incidence of atrocity around the world increases as population growth, urbanization, and scarce resources aggravate ethnic conflict. When human rights abuses are halted anywhere, international troops may have to remain on the ground indefinitely. Intervention, therefore, even when the will and manpower are available, will always be selective.

Our obsession with the Munich debacle over other instances of appeasement shows just how selective we have always been regarding what emergencies are deemed important and what aren't. In 1919, the Western Allies recognized Japan's illegal conquest of China's Shantung Peninsula. They appeased Japan again in 1932, when it began its conquest of Manchuria. This led to Japan's 1937 "Rape of Nanking," where Japanese soldiers "killed, by hand," from 40,000 to 60,000 Chinese civilians using bayonets, machine guns, and kerosene.[19] Yet in heated discussions about Bosnia, Rwanda, and Timor, it was Munich that was usually invoked; not Nanking, even while the latter is still a major unresolved diplomatic issue between Japan and China. The particularity of our collective memories suggests that we will be equally discriminating about future interventions, especially given the limits of our political and military resources, and the enormity of the world and its complex problems.

We will, and should, intervene whenever an overwhelming strategic interest intersects with a moral one, which was the case in the 1930s in both Manchuria and Central Europe, and more recently in Bosnia. But in other cases, our decisions to intervene will be based on a variety of legitimate factors: geography, historical and ethnic patterns, ease of operation, the views of our allies, and the extent of our own determination, which, if sufficient, may override all obstacles. The emergence of an authentic global constabulary force will widen the scope for involvement, but not infinitely.

Christianity is about the moral conquest of the world, while Greek tragedy is about the clash of irreconcilable elements. As Machiavelli cruelly but accurately puts it, progress often comes from hurting others.[20] In deciding where to intervene, policymakers will have to put such difficult truths at the service of our long-range goals; we will have to recognize that while virtue is good, outstanding virtue can be dangerous.[21]

People and their fate matter everywhere. Thus, whenever we generalize about them and fail to intervene, we will be guilty of indifference, ignorance, and political calculation. On the other hand, we cannot be like Conrad's puffing gunboat in *Heart of Darkness*, shelling indiscriminately at the "opaque vastness."[22]

CHAPTER VII

THE GREAT DISTURBERS:
HOBBES AND MALTHUS

In foreign policy, a modest acceptance of fate will often lead to discipline rather than indifference. The realization that we cannot always have our way is the basis of a mature outlook that rests on an ancient sensibility, for tragedy is not the triumph of evil over good so much as the triumph of one good over another that causes suffering. Awareness of that fact leads to a sturdy morality grounded in fear as well as in hope. The moral benefits of fear bring us to two English philosophers who, like Machiavelli, have for centuries disturbed people of goodwill: Hobbes and Malthus.

Thomas Hobbes was born in 1588 and lived to be ninety-one, an astonishing span for his era. Though known to posterity as a gloomy philosopher, he was personally quite genial. Tall and erect in posture, he was active to the end, playing tennis until well past seventy and translating Homer's *Odyssey* and *Iliad* in his eighties.

The son of a vicar who abandoned him when he was four, he was brought up by a prosperous uncle and went to Oxford, where he studied geography, among other subjects. As tutor to a wealthy young man, William Cavendish, Hobbes had the benefit of European travel and the use of a magnificent library, in which he began an intellectual journey that would lead him through the Greek and Latin classics, history, the sciences, and mathematics—all of which he incorporated into several large volumes of philosophy, notably *Leviathan*, as controversial during Hobbes's lifetime as it is now, because of his preference for monarchy over democracy, and his doubt that human beings have the capacity for moral choice. Hobbes also produced a translation of Thucydides' *Peloponnesian War* that is still read today.

Hobbes was influenced by the seething discontent that gripped England in the 1630s, followed by the Civil Wars of 1642–51. Though many of his political themes were already articulated before the anarchy of the 1640s, those terrible events fortified and refined his views.

In 1642, grievances over taxes, monopolies, and the role of the clergy led to warfare between King Charles I and Parliament. Parliament's "New Model Army" swept through the southwest of England, while the rebellious Scots swept through the north. The flight of royalist troops forced Charles to seek refuge with the Scots, who handed him back to his parliamentary enemies. Charles escaped, initiating another orgy of battles won by the New Model Army, which tried and executed him in 1649. Then fighting spread to Ireland, where Catholics and royalists loyal to Charles II—newly crowned in Scotland, and with new Scottish allies—rose up against the parliamentary army. Though Parliament put down the rebellion in Ireland, it failed to prevent Charles II from marching deep into England. But the new king was soon defeated, ending the Civil Wars in 1651.

The lord protector of the new "commonwealth" was Oliver Cromwell, a fiery Puritan who more than two decades earlier had launched the attack on Charles I's bishops that helped ignite the civil war. Cromwell believed that individual Christians could communicate directly with God without the clergy as intermediaries. Cromwell, a genius at organization, had established Parliament's New Model Army, which proved too powerful for Parliament even, leading some of its members to seek help from the Scots against him. It was the split between Parliament and its own army that emboldened the royalists to continue the civil war, despite heavy losses.

After his army disbanded Parliament, Cromwell became a virtual dictator. He tried to replace Parliament with a second legislature, which, because of its radicalism, was known as the Assembly of Saints. It was Cromwell's loyalists, known as Roundheads—because of their close-cropped haircuts—who desecrated bas-relief tombs and church statues, which they considered idols. Cromwell died of malaria in 1658. In 1661, after the restoration of Charles II, his embalmed remains were removed from Westminster Abbey and reburied with those of criminals at Tyburn.

Though Hobbes was in Paris for much of this period, he was in the company of royalist exiles who had fled England for their lives. Thus, like Thucydides and Machiavelli, his philosophy is inseparable from the political turmoil he knew firsthand.

Hobbes relied on history and current events for his philosophy just as Thucydides and Machiavelli did; in them he saw examples of how human beings behave according to their passions. History taught Hobbes that just as vanity and overconfidence can make men blind, fear can make them see clearly, and act morally. According to Hobbes, virtue is rooted in fear. And the "sum of virtue," Hobbes writes, "is to be sociable with them that will be sociable, and formidable to them that will not."[1]

Among the many useful analyses of Hobbes's thinking, perhaps the clearest is *The Political Philosophy of Hobbes: Its Basis and Its Genesis* by the University of Chicago political scientist Leo Strauss, published in 1936.[2] For Strauss and others, Hobbes may be the ultimate constructive pessimist. His view of human nature is exceedingly grim. According to Hobbes, altruism is unnatural, human beings are rapacious, the struggle of every man against every other is the natural condition of humanity, and reason is usually impotent against passion. This view of human nature is the basis for the separation of powers outlined in the Constitution: witness Hamilton's remark that "the passions of men will not conform to the dictates of reason without constraint," and Madison's that "ambition must be made to counteract ambition."[3] In a more general bow to Hobbes, both Hamilton and Madison consistently emphasized the power of irrational motives over ideals. "Men often oppose a thing merely because they have had no agency in planning it," Hamilton writes, "or because it may have been planned by those whom they dislike."[4]

Human beings, Hobbes writes, resemble other animals in that they are constantly exposed to multiple impressions, which elicit never-ending fears and appetites. Since human beings can imagine the future, they are less at the mercy of momentary impressions. Nevertheless, their ability to think about what-comes-next gives them additional hungers and fears, unprecedented in the animal kingdom. Thus, man is "the most cunning, the strongest, and most dangerous animal."[5]

A man's greatest fear, Hobbes tells us, is of violent death: death at the hands of a fellow man. Hobbes says that this "pre-rational" fear is the basis of all morality, since it forces men into "concord" with each other.[6] *But it is a morality of need, not of choice.* Human beings, in order to physically protect themselves, have no choice but to submit themselves to Government, which Hobbes likens to a Leviathan—what God in the Book of Job calls the "king over all the children of pride."[7]

This was not a wholly original view. Aristotle, in the fourth century B.C., had indicated that the city-state comes into existence for the defense of lives and property against criminals.[8] And in the fourteenth century, Ibn Khaldu'n, the Moorish politician and sociologist, defined "royal authority" as that which exercises a "restraining influence" on other men, "for aggressiveness and injustice are in the animal nature of man."[9] What Hobbes did was to elaborate on an old idea.

Because its founding purpose is to keep men from killing each other, the Leviathan is a monopolizer of force. Thus, despotism can be "taken for granted" as the natural state of affairs.[10] Hobbes preferred monarchy to other forms of government because it mirrored the hierarchy of the natural world. Though democracy and other advanced types of regimes are "artificial," they may still succeed, but they require an educated populace, as well as talented elites, to take root.[11]

"Before the names of Just and Unjust can have place," Hobbes famously writes, "there must be some coercive power. . . ."[12] For "where no Covenant hath preceded . . . every man has right to every thing; and consequently, no action can be Unjust."[13] In short, in the violent world of men, an act is immoral only if it is punishable. Without a Leviathan to punish what is Wrong, there can be no escape from the chaos of the state of nature.

In 1995 and 1996, the inhabitants of Freetown, the capital of Sierra Leone, were protected by the presence of South African mercenaries. When the mercenaries left in 1997, there was a military coup that resulted in anarchy and grave human rights violations. The civilian government returned to power only with the help of another group of mercenaries, this time from Great Britain.[14] When those mercenaries left, a ragtag army of substance-abusing teenagers invaded Freetown in December 1998, killing, mutilating, and abducting thousands as order in the capital broke down completely. Two years later, when the same mob-army closed in again on Freetown, the international community dispatched British commandos to protect the capital. Sierra Leone, with no functioning institutions, no economy, and many armed young men, was a replica of the state-of-nature. What was needed was not elections, but a Leviathan, a regime powerful enough to monopolize the use of force, thereby protecting the inhabitants from the lawlessness of armed marauding bands. Just as a despotic regime must precede a liberal one, order must precede democracy, because the State in its original form can emerge only from the *natural state*. It will not help Haiti or the Democratic Republic of the Congo to hold elections if there is no government able to stop violence.

Freedom becomes an issue only after order has been established. "We say that the nature of man is to seek freedom," writes Isaiah

Berlin, "even though very few men in the long life of our race have in fact pursued it, and seem contented to be ruled by others. . . . Why should man alone . . . be classified in terms of what at most small minorities here and there have ever sought for its own sake, still less actively fought for?"[15] Making Hobbes's point more directly is Harvard professor Samuel P. Huntington in his classic *Political Order in Changing Societies:* "The most important political distinction among countries concerns not their form of government but their degree of government. The differences between democracy and dictatorship are less than the differences between those countries whose politics embodies consensus, community, legitimacy, organization, effectiveness, stability, and those countries whose politics is deficient in those qualities."[16]

Hobbes says the fear of violent death (not the fear of punishment for a crime committed) is the basis of conscience, and also of religion. Fear of violent death is a deep and farsighted fear that allows men to comprehend fully the tragedy of life. It is from that realization that men develop the inner convictions that lead them to create civil societies; whereas fear of punishment is a "momentary fear which sees only the next step."[17]

Fear of violent death is the cornerstone of enlightened self-interest. By establishing a state, men replace the fear of violent death—an all-encompassing, mutual fear—with the fear that only those who break the law need face.

Hobbes's concepts are difficult to grasp for the urban middle class, who have long since lost any contact with man's natural state. But however culturally and technologically advanced a society is, it will endure and remain civil only so long as it can in some way imagine man's original condition.

Of course, drugs and biotechnology may change human nature itself in our lifetimes, but it may do so only in the advanced parts of the world, where those in control of such developments will, as always, employ lofty principles in the pursuit of their own self-interest. Moreover, the greater the advances in biotechnology, the less we will fear death; and by Hobbes's reckoning, the more vain and consequently immoral we are likely to become. With more technological development, our passions will become more refined and obsessive, increasing our proclivity for ruthlessness. The further we think we have traveled from the state-of-nature, the more we will need Hobbes to remind us how close by it really is.

Hobbes was influenced by the sciences, but his philosophy rests on his reading of history and his observation of individuals. Perhaps no other philosopher had such a penetrating grasp of the motives underlying the foundation of civil society, which may account for the echo of Hobbes in *The Federalist Papers*. When Madison writes that "the *causes* of faction cannot be removed and that relief is only to be sought in the means of controlling its *effects*," he is echoing Hobbes's view that human beings are disposed to conflict, and the only solution is a higher, controlling force—the key point of Hobbes's *Leviathan*.[18] The Founders had an overriding fear of anarchy. Hamilton provides a grim description of feudalism with its weak executives leading to frequent baronial wars, while Madison defends the cynical expedients employed by Solon, the statesman of ancient Greece, to maintain order in Athens.[19] "A NATION, without a NATIONAL GOVERNMENT," Hamilton writes, "is, in my view, an awful spectacle."[20]

Though Hobbes was opposed to democracy, he was still a liberal who believed that the legitimacy of government derives from the rights of those governed, something which distinguishes him from Machiavelli.[21] Moreover, Hobbes was a modernizer, because at the time of his writing, modernization meant the breakdown of the medieval order through the establishment of a central authority, which he legitimized.[22] *The Federalist Papers* could be defined as an elaboration of Hobbesian truth.[23]

The Founding Fathers begin where Hobbes left off, with the necessity of establishing order to supplant anarchy, and to protect men from one another. From there, the Founders go on to consider how to make the instrument of that order untyrannical. "In framing a government, . . ." Madison writes, "the great difficulty lies in this: you must first enable the government to control the governed; and in the next place oblige it to control itself. A dependence on the people is, no doubt, the primary control on the government; but experience has taught mankind the necessity of auxiliary precautions."[24]

Those precautions—what Madison calls "inventions of prudence"—are the checks and balances that divide the U.S. government into executive, legislative, and judicial spheres, and the legislative branch itself into a Senate and House of Representatives.[25]

But even as the Founders thought less of monarchy than did Hobbes, they were focused on the problem of how passion and self-interest drove men to harm other men. Hence, Madison's hopeful reflection that the future "republic of the United States" would consist of a society "broken into so many parts, interests and classes of citizens, that the rights of the individuals, or of the minority, will be in little danger from interested combinations of the majority"; security, Madison concludes, would be guaranteed by a "multiplicity of interests" and a "multiplicity of sects."[26]

While the Founders wandered a great distance from Hobbes, they never departed from his central thesis: that good government can emerge only from a sly understanding of men's passions. As Madison writes: "[A] nation of philosophers is as little to be expected as the philosophical race of kings wished for by Plato."[27]

Alas, just as the American Revolution is impossible to imagine without Gutenberg's invention of movable type, it is also impossible to imagine without the philosophy of Hobbes and Machiavelli. It was Machiavelli who identified men's need to acquire material provisions as the basis for all conflict. And because the future is unpredictable, a man never knows how much material wealth is sufficient; thus he goes on acquiring, whether he needs to or not. That led Hobbes to outline an impartial, supervisory organ—the State—to peaceably regulate the struggle for possessions.[28] As the first philosopher to distinguish completely the state from society, Hobbes anticipated modern, bureaucratic authority, whose aim, according to both Hobbes and the Founding Fathers, was never to seek the highest good, only the common good.[29]

The Founders adhered to the idea of pagan virtue. Recognizing that faction and struggle are basic to the human condition, they substituted the arenas of party politics and the marketplace for actual battlefields.[30] Like Sparta, the United States would be a "mixed regime" in which the various branches of government struggled against each other, but whereas Sparta was dedicated to war, the

United States—protected by great oceans—would be dedicated to peaceful commerce.[31]

Good government—and, likewise, good foreign policy—will always depend on an understanding of men's passions, which issue from our elemental fears. Both reason and morality, according to Hobbes, are logical responses to the various obstacles and dangers we face in our lives. Thus, philosophy (rational inquiry) is about the resolution of forces, and in foreign policy that leads to the search for order.[32]

Because so many states in the developing world have flimsy institutions, the paramount question in world politics in the early twenty-first century will be the re-establishment of order. This Hobbesian scenario will be aggravated by demographic pressures. While the world's population as a whole is aging, for the next decade or so many societies that are already poor and violent will produce increasingly larger numbers of young men, for whom there will be insufficient job opportunities; these youth bulges will be especially prevalent in places like the West Bank, Gaza, Kenya, Zambia, Pakistan, Egypt, and so on. This brings us to Malthus, the philosopher most associated with the negative consequences of population growth. Like it or not, crises in many countries in the foreseeable future will be Hobbesian and Malthusian ones.

Several years ago, at the headquarters of the U.S. Military's Central Command in Tampa, Florida, I met with CENTCOM's commander in chief, Marine General Anthony Zinni. We discussed emerging threats in the Middle East, the area of CENTCOM's responsibility, and talked about dwindling water resources and population growth, and the challenge those trends posed to various regimes. The other officers and scholars present did not dispute the relevancy of such trends. After all, many of the sites of conflict in recent decades—Indonesia, Haiti, Rwanda, the Gaza Strip, Algeria, Ethiopia, Sierra Leone, Somalia, Kashmir, the Solomon Islands, and so on—had abnormally high rates of population growth, particularly among youth, and resource scarcity prior to outbreaks of violence.

As obvious as that insight may have appeared, it was one we owed ultimately to Thomas Robert Malthus's *An Essay on the Principle of Population, as It Affects the Future Improvement of Society, with Remarks on the Speculations of Mr. Godwin, M. Condorcet, and Other Writers.* Malthus's essay, published in 1798, was a reaction to the optimism of the pre-eminent thinkers of the day, notably William Godwin in England and the Marquis de Condorcet in France, who were buoyed by the approach of a new century and the atmosphere of change and freedom sweeping Europe in the wave of the French Revolution (the Napoleonic Wars were still over the horizon).

Godwin believed that men, guided by reason, were perfectible, and that their rationality would allow them to live peacefully in the future without laws and institutions. In place of the state, he proposed self-governing communities. Condorcet—who greeted enthusiastically the outbreak of the French Revolution only to die in prison as one of its victims—believed, like Godwin, that human beings were capable of infinite progress toward an ultimate perfection, with the destruction of inequality between nations and between classes the result.[33] Malthus countered that human perfection contradicted the laws of nature. This view was supported by Thucydides in the early fifth century B.C., Machiavelli in the sixteenth century, Hobbes in the seventeenth, Edmund Burke and the Founding Fathers in the eighteenth, and Isaiah Berlin and Raymond Aron in the twentieth. Even if the ideal societies envisioned by Godwin and Condorcet came into being, Malthus argued, prosperity would, at least initially, lead people to have more children who would live longer, causing an increase in population that would, in turn, create more complex societies, with sealed-off elites and underclasses. Leisure, Malthus added, would produce as much evil as good. As for human fulfillment, he writes, "The fine silks and cottons, the laces, and other ornamental luxuries of a rich country may contribute very considerably to augment the exchangeable value of its annual produce: yet they contribute but in a very small degree to augment the mass of happiness in the society. . . ."[34]

When Charles Darwin read Malthus's essay in 1838, he announced: "I had at last got a theory by which to work."[35] Darwin saw how the struggle for resources among a growing population might preserve favorable variations and destroy unfavorable ones, leading to the formation of new species. In 1933, John Maynard Keynes wrote of Malthus's essay: "It is profoundly in the English tradition of humane science . . . a tradition marked by a love of truth and a most noble lucidity, by a prosaic sanity free from sentiment or metaphysic, and by an immense disinterestedness and public spirit."[36]

Yet Malthus's specific theory—that population increases geometrically while food supplies increase only arithmetically—was wrong. It was Condorcet who correctly predicted that the tools of the Industrial Revolution would add significantly to agricultural output. Thus, Condorcet exposed the fundamental flaw of Malthus's reasoning: that because the food and energy required for our survival come ultimately from the sun, which will not burn out for several billion years, the methods we can devise for harnessing that energy are virtually limitless.[37]

Still, social theorists may be judged by the questions they stimulate rather than by those they answer. While Condorcet was right, Malthus achieved something greater. Even more so than Adam Smith in *The Wealth of Nations*, Malthus introduced the subject of ecosystems into contemporary political philosophy, thereby immeasurably enriching it. Humankind might be nobler than the apes, but we are still biological. Therefore, our politics—our social relations—Malthus suggested, are affected both by natural conditions and by the densities in which we inhabit the earth.

Malthus was born in 1766 with a harelip and cleft palate, the sixth child of the wealthy and liberal-minded Daniel Malthus. At Cambridge he studied mathematics, history, and philosophy, but partly because of his speech defect, he decided to go into the church and live a somewhat secluded life in the country. Father and son were close, and the younger Malthus, a conservative skeptic, had many friendly debates with his father, who had been influenced by the utopian ideals of Jean-Jacques Rousseau and the French Revolution. Though he disagreed with his conservative son, the elder Malthus was so impressed with the young man's reasoning that he convinced him to put his thoughts to paper.

The essay that resulted from the paternal prod profoundly disturbed the peace. One of the most tranquil and cheerful of men, who never minded interruptions (especially by children, to whom he would give his full attention), Malthus was humiliated by the literary elite of the day, including Wordsworth, Coleridge, and Shelley.[38] Shelley called Malthus "a eunuch and a tyrant" and "the apostle of the rich" because of his matter-of-fact statement based on empirical observation that "we cannot possibly expect to exclude riches and poverty from society."[39] In *A Christmas Carol*, Dickens's Ebenezer Scrooge, who had remarked that the poor might as well die and "decrease the surplus population," satirized Malthus.[40] Friedrich Engels called Malthus's essay a "repulsive blasphemy against man and nature."[41]

Malthus's geometric-arithmetic theory of how poverty results from excess population was only an example of his larger point about the relationship between social peace and food supplies. Defending Malthus in 1864, John Stuart Mill notes that "every candid reader knows that Mr. Malthus laid no stress on this unlucky attempt to give numerical precision to things which do not admit it, and every person of reason must see that it is wholly superfluous to his argument."[42] In fact, Malthus revised his *Essay* six times, retreating from his arithmetic argument while upholding the central thesis: that population expands to the limits imposed by its means of subsistence. And as increases in food supply led to increases in population (at least in the pre- and early-industrial societies to which Malthus refers) that deduction was reasonable.

Where food is scarce, whether because of prices, maldistribution, political malfeasance, or drought, conflict or disease has often resulted. In Ethiopia and Eritrea in the 1980s, I saw firsthand how a drought caused partly by weather patterns and the overuse of soil by a growing population intensified ethnic conflict, which, in turn, was manipulated by a murderous Ethiopian regime. People don't hold up signs that say, "Now that there are so many of us, we will act irrationally." Exploding demographics do not by themselves cause unrest; they aggravate existing ethnic and political tensions, as in Rwanda and the Indonesian archipelago, for example. Malthus writes that there would always be "vice and misery," and that "moral evil is absolutely necessary to the production of moral excellence," because morality requires the conscious choice of good over evil. "Upon this idea," he goes on, "the being that has seen moral evil and has felt disapprobation and disgust at it is essentially different from the being that has seen only good."[43] Without evil there can be no virtue. To wit, the willingness to confront evil with force at propitious moments is the mark of a great statesman.

Though we now take these observations for granted, more than any other figure of the Enlightenment, Malthus continues to stir resentment. Humanists reject him because of his implied determinism: he treats humankind as a species rather than as a body of self-willed individuals. And there are those, such as the late classical economist Julian Simon, who assume that human ingenuity will solve every resource problem, neglecting to consider that such ingenuity often arrives too late to forestall political upheaval: the English Revolution of 1640, the French Revolution of 1789, the European revolts of 1848, and numerous rebellions in the Chinese and Ottoman empires all occurred against a background of high population growth and food shortages.[44]

Malthus—the first philosopher to focus on the political effects of poor soils, famine, disease, and the quality of life among the poor—is an irritant because he has defined the most important debate of the first half of the twenty-first century. As the human population rises from 6 billion to 10 billion before it is predicted to level off, testing the planet's environment as never before—with a billion people going to bed hungry and violence (both political and criminal) chronic throughout poor parts of the globe—the word *Malthusian* will be heard with increasing frequency in the years to come.[45]

This situation can only be exacerbated by global warming, which a U.N. scientific team believes will cause massive flooding, disease, and drought that will interrupt subsistence farming in many parts of the world. Global warming, as a phenomenon of the physical world, is another example of Malthus's tenet that ecosystems have a direct impact on politics.[46]

Even were we to leave global warming aside, policymakers will have to confront the danger of great, politically explosive urban populations inhabiting flood and earthquake zones for the first time in history, whether in the Indian subcontinent, the Nile Delta, the tectonically unstable Caucasus, Turkey, and Iran, or China, where two thirds of the population producing 70 percent of the industrial output live below the flood level of major rivers.[47] And as science learns to predict weather and other natural events, policymakers will want to know what the future holds for such ecologically and politically fragile areas. This will add another Malthusian element to foreign policy.

If Malthus is wrong, then why is it necessary to prove him wrong again and again, every decade and every century? Perhaps because, at some fundamental level, a gnawing fear exists that Malthus may just be right. The sight of that fragile, bluish gem floating in space, first seen by the Apollo astronauts in 1969—followed by fears of global warming, pollution, ozone depletion, suburban sprawl, re-source shortages, and population growth—begot the realization that for our ecosystem to survive and prosper, certain limits to growth should be observed: limits that Malthus was the first to recognize.

CHAPTER VIII

THE HOLOCAUST,

REALISM, AND KANT

In recent decades, unprecedented affluence has led to unprecedented altruism and idealism, complicating our reaction to the difficult truths revealed by philosophers like Hobbes and Malthus. Behind this altruism and idealism is the specter of the Holocaust. Because foreign policy is, ultimately, the extension of a country's domestic inclinations and conditions, it is necessary to say something about it.

At the turn of the twenty-first century, the Holocaust has become more than a Jewish memory. It is taught by law in the public schools. Annual commemorative ceremonies are held in the Capitol Rotunda. The federal government pays for most of the upkeep of the U.S. Holocaust Museum near the Jefferson Memorial in Washington, D.C. Peter Novick, in his path-breaking book *The Holocaust in American Life,* calls it "the emblematic atrocity," the most likely "criterion by which we decide what horrors command our attention" and what do not.

The Holocaust grew to vast significance not only because of its intrinsic horror but also because of specific conditions in post–World War II American life. In the 1950s, as Jews assimilated rapidly into American society, American Jewish organizations rarely mentioned the Holocaust; they chose to appear part of the patriotic mainstream at a time when Jews like Ethel and Julius Rosenberg figured prominently in Cold War espionage investigations, and anti-Semitism was still rife.[1] Growing up in the 1950s, the movie director Steven Spielberg learned little about the Holocaust from a popular culture that prized consensus and assimilation. Spielberg said that making *Schindler's List* was "an outgrowth of his increasing Jewish awareness" that occurred only in the 1970s.[2]

It was actually in the 1960s that the Holocaust began to be transformed from an assemblage of searing family memories to a totemic event. William L. Shirer's 1960 bestseller, *The Rise and Fall of the Third Reich,* and the trial of Adolf Eichmann in 1961 may have played less of a role in this process than the sixties themselves—a time of social upheaval that led, by the 1970s, to "an era devoted to diversity . . . the elaboration of ethnicity and the exploration of one's heritage," in the words of the Holocaust scholar Hilene Flanzbaum.[3] The Holocaust soon became the defining narrative of a generation of Jews who had become part of America's secular mainstream, and thus required a new badge of identification with their ethnic forebears, now that both Orthodox and Yiddish culture had largely been lost.

The Holocaust influenced—and was influenced by—the cult of victimhood that flourished in the aftermath of the sixties, in which women, blacks, Native Americans, Armenians, and others fortified their identities through public references to past oppression. That process was tied to Vietnam, a war in which the photographs of civilian victims—the little girl fleeing napalm, for example—"displaced traditional images of heroism."[4]

The Holocaust took on further meaning following the West's victory in the Cold War, when the failure of communism focused increased attention on the mass murders committed by Stalin and Mao. Then came the atrocities in Bosnia and Rwanda, with their eerie similarities to the Holocaust, especially the bureaucratic death apparatus. Identification with the Holocaust taught us to see the victims in those places as not just a mass of white or black bodies, but as individuals, each with a life story. The Nazis' unimaginable assault on human rights led to an unparalleled concern with human rights.

But it was also the unprecedented physical and material security evinced by the suburbs in the decades following World War II that provided many Americans—young people especially—with the means to engage in the highest degree of altruism: the kind not limited to one's family or ethnic group, but extending to all humanity.[5] Perhaps for the first time in history, there was a generation without direct experience of poverty, depression, war, invasion, and other terrors that human beings for ages have regarded as ordinary elements of daily life: the Cold War, because it was cold, was also abstract; while the Vietnam War, to a significant degree, was fought by the less affluent classes. As the sixties' youth rebellion showed, this suburban cocoon bred both conformity and a rarefied idealism—a desire to transcend international politics rather than engage in them, with the unsatisfactory moral compromises which that entailed.

Particularly at the end of the Cold War, many believed that we could escape at last from the human condition, with democracy, free market capitalism, and a new respect for the rights of the individual replacing power politics and the self-interest of nations and other groups.[6] The collapse of the Berlin Wall led to the hope that all humanity was marching toward the same progressive horizon. It was a notion that Isaiah Berlin and Raymond Aron—echoing Thucydides, Machiavelli, Hobbes, and the Founding Fathers—branded unrealistic, because such an ideal lay outside history, which is never free of human division and conflict.[7]

Indeed, the concern of the Republican Right with "values" and that of liberals with "humanitarian intervention" may be less a sign of a higher morality following the defeat of communism than of the luxury afforded by domestic peace and prosperity. In her acclaimed fictional memoir of the emperor Hadrian, the novelist Marguerite Yourcenar speculates that in the second century A.D. the increased freedoms for women in Rome were the result of good times, not of civic character.[8] Though the expansion of wealth in the United States may offer the prospect of greater altruism, poverty and insecurity—combined with population growth and urbanization in the least developed parts of the world—will generate more cruelty, because it will confine altruism to the level of national and subnational groups.

We need to keep in mind that the new era of human rights that policymakers and the media have declared is neither completely new nor completely real. Ever since Cicero, statesmen have proclaimed moral principles for a "human community" that no dictator has the right to annul.[9] In 1880, Britain's prime minister, William Gladstone, affronted by Benjamin Disraeli's calculated manipulation of power, affirmed that Christian decency and human rights would henceforth govern foreign policy. Gladstone spoke of "a new law of nations" that would protect "the sanctity of life" even in "the hill villages of Afghanistan."[10] Of course, that was not to be. Following the First World War, President Woodrow Wilson proclaimed (in words much like Gladstone's) another era of human rights, which also did not materialize. In 1928, sixty-two nations—including Japan, Germany, Great Britain, France, and the United States—signed the Kellogg-Briand Pact outlawing war, and relied on public opinion to enforce it. "Those critics who scoff at it," wrote Secretary of State Henry L. Stimson, "have not accurately appraised the evolution in world opinion since the Great War."[11] But principles are usually not self-implementing, as Henry Kissinger reminds us, and World War II followed.[12]

After the Yalta Conference, President Roosevelt declared "the end . . . of unilateral action, the exclusive alliances, the spheres of influence, the balance of power, and all the other expedients that have been tried for centuries—and have always failed."[13] Instead, he proposed a "universal organization," the United Nations.[14] A few weeks later, in early 1945, Stalin created a sphere of influence that would hold Central and Eastern Europe captive for over four decades. Sensing the danger, Churchill tried and failed to convince the Americans to grab Berlin and Prague ahead of the advancing Red Army.

Today, in the spirit of Gladstone, Wilson, Stimson, and Roosevelt, a new era of human rights has been declared, even as globalization, for all its virtues, proves also to be a force for bad urbanization, economic inequality, and heightened ethnic awareness, responsible in some instances for fueling political extremism and the consequent disregard of human rights.

Values, however universal in principle, will always require muscle and self-interest to enforce. In the 1990s, the Vatican, the Eastern Orthodox Patriarchate, and the United Nations reacted to war crimes in the Balkans not with unequivocal condemnation but with vacillation—exactly as similar august parties had reacted to the crimes of the Nazis. To expect human beings and organizations to think about the interests of others before their own is to ask them to deny their own instincts for self-preservation. Even with relief charities and other nongovernmental organizations, self-interest comes first: they lobby for intervention in areas where they are active, rather than in others where they are less so. One reason the media gave so much attention to Bosnia and comparatively little to concurrent ethnic atrocities in Abkhazia, South Ossetia, and Nagorno-Karabakh was that relief charities—sometimes the media's best sources—were more active in the Balkans than in the Caucasus. Because the world is full of cruelty and even our own good intentions are sometimes less than they seem, the moral lessons of the Holocaust—that "emblematic atrocity"—will be hard to apply to our satisfaction in many places.

It is geography that has helped sustain our prosperity and which may be ultimately responsible for America's pan-humanistic altruism. As John Adams notes, "[T]here is no special providence for Americans, and their nature is the same with that of others."[15] The historian John Keegan explains that Britain and America could champion freedom only because the sea protected them "from the landbound enemies of liberty." The militarism and pragmatism of continental Europe to which Americans have always felt superior is the result of geography, not character. Competing states and empires adjoined each other on a crowded continent. European nations could never withdraw across an ocean in the event of a military miscalculation. Thus, their foreign policies could not be grounded by a universalist morality, and they remained well armed against each other until dominated by an American hegemon after World War II. Alexander Hamilton says that had Britain not been an island, its military establishment would have been just as overbearing as those of continental Europe, and Britain "would in all probability" have become "a victim to the absolute power of a single man."[16]

Vast oceans have given Americans the protection necessary to advance universalist principles. But in an increasingly smaller world, in which the Middle East and sub-Saharan Africa will be as close to us in military terms as Prussia was to Ottoman Turkey, the room for miscalculation will continue to diminish. Thus, a variant of European-style pragmatism may encroach upon the American public and its policymakers. Wilsonian morality is attractive only so long as Americans think they are invulnerable. The public's desire to withdraw from our humanitarian mission in Somalia in 1993 after a small number of casualties and the weak public support for the air war in Kosovo in 1999 could be harbingers of that trend. Isolationism was always inseparable from our idealism because if we could not change the world, we could always withdraw from it, as we did after World War I. But as technology overcomes oceanic distances, the duo of isolationism and idealism is being replaced by active engagement and realism. More than in the past even, prudence will discipline our passions.

—

The defining characteristic of realism is that international relations are governed by different moral principles than domestic politics— a notion justified by the writings of Thucydides, Machiavelli, Hobbes, Churchill, and others. The need for this distinction was underscored by the birth of modern capitalism itself: the impetus for Richelieu's *raison d'état*. What, after all, is modern capitalism but *raison d'économie*?[17] The rationality required to manage the complex economic operations of a bureaucratized French state that emerged in the early seventeenth century gradually supplanted the individual arbitrariness of feudal barons, providing the context for Richelieu's comparable pragmatism in foreign affairs. George Kennan notes that private morality is not a criterion for judging the behavior of states or for comparing one state with another. "Here other criteria, sadder, more limited, more practical, must be allowed to prevail."[18] The historian Arthur Schlesinger Jr. advises that in foreign affairs morality lies not in "the trumpeting of moral absolutes," but in "fidelity to one's own sense of honor and decency"; and in "the assumption that other nations have legitimate traditions, interests, values and rights of their own."[19]

Ethnic killing in Bosnia and Rwanda offended our "sense of honor and decency." But our late entry into Bosnia and our failure to intervene in Rwanda illustrate the difficulty of applying private morality to foreign policy. Whether one supported intervention or not in those instances—and even admitting that more could have been done at little cost or risk, especially in Rwanda—it was, nevertheless, legitimate for our policymakers to worry about the United States getting bogged down, Vietnam-style, in the Balkans and in east-central Africa. In October 1993, six months before the crisis in Rwanda, eighteen American soldiers had been killed and dozens more wounded in Somalia, in the worst firefight since the Vietnam War. Had something similar occurred in Rwanda, the American public's appetite for armed intervention might have evaporated, complicating our later interventions in 1995 in Bosnia and in 1999 in Kosovo, and with negative consequences elsewhere.

The impossibility of perfect outcomes is noted by the late American historian Barbara Tuchman in her analysis of the West's appeasement of Japan in the early 1930s:

> Statesmen are not seers and their actions are taken in contemporary context with no view over the hill. The working out of a crisis takes place in stages without history's advantage of seeing the event whole. . . . It is doubtful if any stage of the Manchurian crisis could have happened otherwise, for in the course of the process there were no likely alternatives that could have been seized, no might-have-beens just barely missed. Some periods breed greatness, others feebleness. The Manchurian crisis was one of the causative events of history born, not of tragic "ifs," but of the inherent limitations of men and states.[20]

China is also a case of clashing foreign and domestic principles. When the most liberal Chinese regime of the twentieth century reformed its economy but not its authoritarian system, the administration of the elder George Bush, as well as the Clinton administration by its second term, did not seek to impose upon China our own moral values; rather, they promoted them indirectly through increased trade, which benefited our own economy and helped stabilize American-Chinese relations. Limiting (but by no means eliminating) the emphasis on human rights in our policy toward a great Asian power was a good illustration of Kennan's realism, which is moral, even if it is not Judeo-Christian.

In the twenty-first century realism is appropriate to a Hobbesian world in which there is no global Leviathan monopolizing the use of force in order to punish the Unjust. Though the world's preeminent power, the United States can punish the Unjust only occasionally, or else it would be permanently overextended in its dealings with regional hegemons like China, as well as permanently engaged in small wars, and its power would consequently diminish. The same holds for NATO and other organizations. The international criminal court in The Hague is a bold attempt to address this Hobbesian dilemma. But the court (along with other supranational authorities) is only the start of a process to create an international Leviathan. The world is still a place where various powers representing different values and different degrees of altruism compete—often violently.

Whether in antiquity or in the post–Cold War world, the central question of foreign affairs remains: *Who can do what to whom?*[21] The phrase "balance of power" is less a theory of international relations than a description of it.

President Theodore Roosevelt identified the national interest with the balance of power. He established the Panama Canal Zone in 1903, an economic protectorate over the Dominican Republic in 1905, and occupied Cuba in 1906 in order to strengthen the United States in its own hemisphere against the thrust of European influence in a more interconnected world. After Hitler upset the balance of power in Europe, Churchill, a fierce anti-Communist, sought an alliance with Stalin to redress the imbalance. President Richard Nixon, another fierce anti-Communist, followed Churchill's example three

decades later when he sought an alliance with China against the Soviet Union, in order to alter the global balance of power in America's
favor.[22] The 1995 Dayton peace accords that stopped the genocide in
Bosnia might have been impossible if the United States hadn't first
restored the balance of power in the former Yugoslavia, by arming
Croatian troops against Serbia. As it says in the *Chan-kuo Ts'e*, the
book of wisdom from third century B.C. China: "[I]f your majesty
would become Hegemon he must . . . use the pivot of the empire to
threaten Ch'u and Chao. When Chao is strong, Ch'u will cleave to
you. When Ch'u is strong, Chao will cleave to you. When both have
attached themselves to you then Ch'i will be afraid. . . ."[23]

As long as there is no Leviathan to hold sway over the countries
of the world, power struggles will continue to define international
politics and a global civil society will remain out of reach. Democracy and globalization are partial solutions at best. Historically,
democracies have been as prone to war as other regimes.[24] The late
Oxford classicist Maurice Bowra writes: "Athens provides a signal
refutation of the optimistic delusion that democracies are not bel-
licose or avid of empire."[25] Growing economic interdependence at
the beginning of the twentieth century did not prevent World
War I, whereas the United States and the Soviet Union remained
at peace even though there was little commerce between them.[26]
Economic interdependence creates its own conflicts, while new
democracies in places with weak institutions and ethnic rivalries
are often volatile. Here, again, is Alexander Hamilton, the most
acute voice of the American Revolution:

> Have there not been as many wars founded upon commercial
> motives since that has become the prevailing system of nations,
> as were before occasioned by the cupidity of territory or domin-

ion? Has not the spirit of commerce, in many instances, administered new incentives to the appetite, both for the one and for the other? Let experience, the least fallible guide of human opinions, be appealed to for an answer to these inquiries.[27]

Consequently, realists believe that while human rights are, in theory, advanced by democracy and economic integration, in practice they are advanced by resolving power relationships in ways that allow for more predictable punishment of the Unjust. Of course, that often involves both democratization and free trade, but not always. For in human affairs, moral questions are often linked to questions of power.

Take Serbia in the 1990s: its cruelty toward civilians in Bosnia and Kosovo was in some respects comparable to that of Russia's in Chechnya, to Armenia's in Nagorno-Karabakh, to Indonesia's in East Timor, to the Indian army's in Kashmir, to the Revolutionary United Front's in Sierra Leone, to Abkhazia's in Georgia, to that of rebel groups in the Congo, and so forth. But Russia, Armenia, and India were all democratic regimes at the time they committed their atrocities. And while the arguments for Western intervention in Bosnia and Kosovo were largely moral, what bolstered these moral arguments were, in fact, issues of power. Unlike Congo, Kashmir, or other places in Africa and Asia, the former Yugoslavia had a significant strategic impact on European security and the future of NATO. The former Yugoslavia was also susceptible to military pressure to a degree that other troubled places were not. When reports surfaced of massive atrocities committed by Russian troops against civilians in Chechnya, the same officials in the Clinton administration who had so forcefully advanced moral arguments for intervention in Kosovo suddenly went mute. Unlike Serbia, which could be bombed with impunity, Russia was a major power with a nuclear arsenal.

In Pakistan, I saw firsthand how the change in the internal balance of power had improved the human rights situation, even though a military regime had replaced a democratic one in October 1999. Karachi, a city of 14 million that had seen thousands of deaths because of intercommunal violence, became more peaceful because the military could play the role of Leviathan more successfully than the democratically elected civilians. The military government was also able to speak out against such abhorrent tribal practices as "blasphemy laws" and "honor killings" to a degree that democratic prime ministers, fearful of radical Moslem clerics, could not. The military, at least initially, did not intimidate journalists to the extent that previous civilian prime ministers had. And it could advance the cause of local democracy because it had greater influence over tribal leaders than the civilian politicians.

Ultimately, the Pakistani military failed to build the foundation of a civil society, but it was in a better position to try because the coup leader, General Pervez Musharraf, had both more power and more "virtue" than his civilian predecessors. A devotee of Turkey's progressive founder, Mustafa Kemal Atatürk, General Musharraf was by all accounts the most liberal Pakistani ruler in decades, though unelected.

Nevertheless, while international relations are ultimately questions of power, such a realization is dangerous unless used to advance what Schlesinger calls "honor and decency," a concept that ultimately implies the synthesis of pagan and Judeo-Christian virtue. As Jacques Barzun writes: "[I]t seems bad history to keep referring today to 'our Judaeo-Christian heritage.' Pagan or Graeco-Roman ought to be added to the phrase...."[28]

Though throughout this essay I have emphasized the distinction between pagan and Judeo-Christian values, there is also considerable overlap, and not just because of the moral philosophy of Cicero and Plutarch. Some versions of Christianity are quite compatible with foreign policy realism. Richelieu and Bismarck were associated, respectively, with Catholic and Lutheran pietism, which combines personal piety with a healthy suspicion of religious theology and rationalism.[29] Both men were devout Christians who believed that the irrational passions of their fellow humans were sufficiently wicked to require Hobbesian methods to ensure order. Saint Augustine, too, in his *City of God,* as Garry Wills explains, shows a realist approach to society absent in traditional liberal views of the world. Whereas "liberalism can do nothing but condemn in frustrated noncomprehension" such "irrational" bonds of tribe and ethnicity, Augustine finds that while such bonds do not contribute to the love of God and perfect justice, they may still foster social cohesion, something that is also a good.[30] And, of course, in the twentieth century there was Reinhold Niebuhr, the Protestant theologian and Cold Warrior who espoused the doctrine of "Christian Realism."

What all these men were groping for, it seems, was a way to use pagan, public morality to advance—albeit indirectly—private, Judeo-Christian morality. Put in our own terms, human rights are ultimately and most assuredly promoted by the preservation and augmentation of American power.

> *We hold these truths to be self-evident, that all men are created equal, that they are endowed by their Creator with certain unalienable Rights, that among these are Life, Liberty, and the pursuit of Happiness.*

At about the time that Thomas Jefferson wrote those words for the Declaration of Independence, a professor who held the chair of logic and metaphysics at the University of Königsberg in East Prussia, Immanuel Kant, began work on a series of books proving that such rights were, indeed, "unalienable," and as basic to the needs of humankind as food and water.

Kant was born in 1724 in Königsberg and died there in 1804. He came from a poor, devoutly religious family and attended parochial school, where he developed an aversion to organized religion. He entered the University of Königsberg at sixteen, where he would spend his entire life: as an undergraduate and postgraduate in the natural sciences, as a lecturer, and finally as a professor from the age of forty-six, when his serious writing began. He never married or traveled. For Kant, experience counted for little compared to the life of the mind, and his work is a reflection of this priority.

Kant lies outside the tradition of Thucydides, Livy, Machiavelli, Hobbes, and others for whom history was the raw material of philosophy. Like Plato, Kant seeks the perfect society, one based on reason rather than on experience. Kant cannot help us deal with the world as it is. But he can help us better appreciate the values for which we fight.

Kant's paragraphs have so much going on in them that they often have the intensity of poetry. The *Critique of Pure Reason* is his most famous work, but the *Groundwork of the Metaphysics of Morals,* which followed naturally from the *Critique,* is more germane to our purpose.[31]

While realists admire Hobbes for his analysis of humankind as it is, Kant is admired because he shows how much better humankind can be. Indeed, his essay on "Perpetual Peace" suggests a wily historical mechanism for ensuring moral progress.[32] But the two philosophers are not really in opposition. Kant can also be an acute observer of human motivation. He writes that even when morality appears to be the grounds for our actions, "it cannot be inferred with certainty that no covert impulse of self-love, under the mere pretense of" morals, is not the real cause of our actions, "for we like to flatter ourselves by falsely attributing to ourselves a nobler motive. . . ."[33] Since "the most strenuous self-examination" still won't allow us to see "entirely behind" our own motivations and those of others, proof of moral action can be deduced only by reason, never from mere experience.[34] Because he knows that selfish calculations lie behind so many so-called moral arguments, Kant criticizes "political moralism"—attacking one's adversary as immoral merely because of a political difference.[35]

Like Hobbes, Kant knows that our fears and appetites cause us to act irrationally. But then he asks: are there not laws that indicate how we "*ought*" to act?[36] To prove that there are such laws, he engages in reasoning unconstrained and unprejudiced by experience.

Kant says that when we act in a way that we would want without contradiction everyone else to act, then it is a "*universal law,*" which no government has the right to deny.[37] To pin down what he means, he describes behavior that while defensible, could not be made universal without grave contradictions:

- Consider a man whose life is full of troubles that lead him to despair. Knowing, therefore, that in all probability the future holds more unhappiness than happiness, he decides out of self-love to kill himself. While justifying such an action, Kant notes that suicide could not be a universal law because the general purpose of life cannot be to destroy itself.

- Consider another man who needs to borrow money in order to survive, but knows that he can never repay it. Out of desperation, he borrows the money anyway. But if everyone were to do that, Kant says, then no one would lend money anymore. So it could not be a universal law.

- Finally, consider a man in fortunate circumstances who just wants to be left alone, and so does not help or harm those in dire need. But even he, Kant explains, cannot wish, without contradiction, for everyone always to act thus, since there would be moments in life when he would require the goodwill of others.

Kant, like Hobbes, does not claim that immorality is irrational; contradictions emerge only when we attempt to make immoral or amoral behavior universal.[38] He shows that the only behavior we could ever wish without contradiction for all to adopt is based on goodwill. Goodwill has intrinsic value even if it doesn't lead to good results; thus, its value is not dependent on experience. To act with goodwill means seeing each man or woman as "an end in itself," and not merely a "*means.*"[39] Kant says that human beings who treat each other as ends rather than as means are free men. A free man acts according to his principles rather than according to his fears or appetites, for it is such fears and appetites that are the external forces constricting our freedom.

What if goodwill leads to disastrous results? Weren't some of the appeasers at least partly motivated by goodwill? And is each man, including Hitler, really an end in himself, to be treated kindly? Of course not. Kant does not deny the existence of evil; rather, he emphasizes that precisely because the world of politics is so messy, moral philosophy cannot depend on what happens in it, otherwise men would have no ideals. And without ideals there would be no basis for the human rights outlined, for example, in the Declaration of Independence: rights that are indisputable because, like the Founders, we wish them without contradiction to be universal.

While different moral value systems may coexist, Kant shows that there are still universal principles worth struggling for—something we know only too well because of the Holocaust.

However, unlike Hobbes, Machiavelli, Thucydides, and Sun-Tzu, Kant provides little practical advice for dealing with a world governed by passion, irrationality, and periodic evil—a world where nations with different historical experiences, such as the United States and China, have legitimate disputes about how to advance the welfare of their citizenries. Thus, a statesman must employ the wisdom of these other philosophers in order to reach the goals outlined by Kant.

Kant symbolizes a morality of intention rather than of consequences, a morality of abstract justice rather than of actual result. He cares about the goodness or badness of a rule, while politics is often about the goodness or badness of a specific act in a specific circumstance, since the same rule might produce good results in one situation and bad results in another. Kant's subject is pure integrity, while politics deals with justification, for if an act is justifiable by its likely results, no matter how sordid some of the inner motivations behind it, some measure of integrity is still inherent in the decision-making process. As Machiavelli says, in an imperfect world men bent on doing good—and who have responsibility for the welfare of a great many others—must know occasionally how to be bad, and to savor it. Franklin Roosevelt might not have accomplished what he did were he not naturally devious. Statesmanship demands a morality of consequence. A statesman must be able to *think the unthinkable.* If he has to operate in an insane environment, such as Serbia under Slobodan Milosevic or Iraq under Saddam Hussein, then "it is insanity to carry the decorum of sanity into it."[40] In October 1998 in Belgrade, Milosevic remarked to U.S. envoy Richard Holbrooke that the United States wasn't crazy enough to bomb Serbia; Holbrooke replied that yes, perhaps *we were crazy enough.* Holbrooke's approval of a calculated insanity signified a morality of consequence. Such a Churchillian morality is comfortable with making the best of a bad job.

Of course, if statesmen pursued only a morality of consequence, they would drown in cynicism and deceit. They should at least consider how, in Kant's words, they *ought* to act: for in a world completely absent of a morality of intent, few would tell the truth or keep their promises.[41] But the fact that there are dangers inherent in a morality of consequence does not mean that it shouldn't predominate in statesmanship. "The only yardstick of advantage," says Cicero, "is moral right."[42] But that is true only overall. Though the West's moral advantage over the East Bloc was decisive in the Cold War, faced with the reality of Soviet aggression it was forced to use tactics such as espionage, the deployment of nuclear weapons, and supporting unpleasant regimes.

While a foreign policy with no moral intent will be cynical, a policy that seeks to guide, justify, and glorify its every action with moral imperatives risks being extremist, for zealotry often goes hand in hand with incorruptibility. That is also the problem with faith. It is not that religion is bad, Machiavelli explains, but that religion leads to extremism when its otherworldliness impinges too much on worldly affairs. The separation of private ethics from politics, begun by Machiavelli among others, and completed by Hobbes, laid the foundation for a diplomacy free from the otherworldly absolutism of the medieval church. We must be careful not to return to such absolutism, for if there is such a thing as progress in politics, it has been the evolution from religious virtue to secular self-interest.[43]

CHAPTER IX

THE WORLD OF ACHILLES:

ANCIENT SOLDIERS,

MODERN WARRIORS

Nothing is great, writes Seneca, "which is not at the same time calm." Gladiators, he goes on to say, "are protected by skill but left defenseless by anger."[1]

More than in any previous epoch, perhaps, the statesman of the future will need to control his emotions, for there will be much to be angry about. Groups that refuse to play by our rules will constantly be committing outrages. Overreaction will exact a terrible price, as technology brings us closer, for example, to the Middle East than Europe ever was. Every diplomatic move will also be a military one, as the artificial separation between the civilian and military command structures that has been a feature of contemporary democracies continues to dissolve. We will revert to the unified leaderships of the ancient and early-modern worlds—what Socrates and Machiavelli recognized as a basic truth of all political systems, whatever the labels those systems claim for themselves.

The split between civilian and military commands emerged

only in the nineteenth century with the professionalization of modern European armies. In part because the Cold War went on for so long, it created a military establishment too vast and well informed to retreat to the margins of policymaking. The chairman of the Joint Chiefs of Staff is now a veritable member of the president's cabinet. The regional commanders in chief of the Middle East, Europe, the Pacific, and the Americas are the modern-day equals of Roman proconsuls, with budgets twice that of the Cold War era, even as State Department and other civilian foreign policy budgets have dwindled.[2]

What will magnify this trend is the commingling of military and civilian high-technology systems, which increasingly puts the military at the mercy of civilian experts, and vice versa. The short, limited wars and rescue operations with which we shall be engaged will go unsanctioned by Congress and the citizenry; so, too, will pre-emptive strikes against the computer networks of our adversaries and other defense-related measures that in many instances will be kept secret. Collaboration between the Pentagon and corporate America is necessary, and will grow. Going to war will be less and less a democratic decision.

In an age when it took weeks to mobilize and transport armored divisions across the seas, it was possible for American presidents to consult the people and Congress about doing so. In the future, when combat brigades can be inserted anywhere in the world in ninety-six hours and entire divisions in 120 hours, and with the majority of our military actions lightning air and computer strikes, the decision to use force will be made autocratically by small groups of civilians and general officers, the differences between them fading as time goes on.[3] Already, the difference in knowledge between generals who operate almost as politicians and civilian specialists in defense policy is often insignificant.

While international law grows in significance through trade organizations and human rights tribunals, it will play less of a role in the conduct of war because war will increasingly be unconventional and undeclared, and fought within states rather than between them. The concept of "international law" promulgated by Hugo Grotius in seventeenth-century Holland, in which all sovereign states are treated as equal and war is justified only in defense of sovereignty, is fundamentally utopian. The boundaries between peace and war are often unclear, and international agreements are kept only if the power and self-interest are there to sustain them.[4] In the future, do not expect wartime justice to depend on international law; as in ancient times, this justice will depend upon the moral fiber of military commanders themselves, whose roles will often be indistinguishable from those of civilian leaders.

The *ancientness* of future wars has three dimensions: the character of the enemy, the methods used to contain and destroy him, and the identity of those beating the war drums.

The national security analyst Lieutenant Colonel Ralph Peters writes that American soldiers "are brilliantly prepared to defeat other soldiers. Unfortunately," he goes on, "the enemies we are likely to face . . . will not be 'soldiers,' " with the discipline and professionalism which that word implies in the West, but " 'warriors'—erratic primitives of shifting allegiance, habituated to violence, with no stake in civil order."[5]

There have always been warriors who, in Homer's words, "call up the wild joy of war. . . ."[6] But the collapse of Cold War empires and the disorder it engendered—along with the advance of technology and low-end urbanization—has provoked the breakdown of families and the renewal of cults and blood ties, including a more militant Islam and Hinduism. The result is the birth of a warrior class as cruel as ever, and better armed. It embraces armies of murderous teenagers in West Africa, Russian and Albanian mafiosi, Latin American drug kingpins, West Bank suicide bombers, and associates of Osama bin Laden who communicate by e-mail. Like Achilles and the ancient Greeks harassing Troy, the thrill of violence substitutes for the joys of domesticity and feasting. Achilles exclaims,

> You talk of food?
> I have no taste for food—what I really crave
> is slaughter and blood and the choking groans of men![7]

Today's warriors come often from the hundreds of millions of unemployed young males in the developing world, angered by the income disparities that accompany globalization. Globalization is Darwinian. It means economic survival of the fittest—those groups and individuals that are disciplined, dynamic, and ingenious will float to the top, while cultures that do not compete well technologically will produce an inordinate number of warriors. I saw firsthand the creation of warriors at Islamic schools in Pakistani slums: the children of those shantytowns had no moral or patriotic identity except that which their religious instructors gave them. An age of chemical and biological weapons is perfectly suited for religious martyrdom.

Warriors are also ex-convicts, ethnic and national "patriots," shadowy arms and drug entrepreneurs awash in cynicism, and failed military men—cashiered officers of formerly Communist and Third World armies. The wars in the Balkans and the Caucasus in the 1990s featured all of these types reborn as war criminals. Whether in Russia, Iraq, or Serbia, nationalism in our age is, Colonel Peters notes, simply a secular form of fundamentalism. Both arise from a sense of collective grievance and historical failure, real or imaginary, and preach a lost golden age. Both dehumanize their adversaries and equate mercy with weakness. Thus, while there are enormous differences between, say, a Radovan Karadzic and an Osama bin Laden, neither plays by our rules; both are warriors.

Hitler was a warrior, a prototypal skinhead with a mustache who wrested control of an advanced industrial state. Anyone who assumes that rational economic incentives determine the future of world politics should read *Mein Kampf*. None of the warriors we have seen since the fall of the Berlin Wall have presented a comparable strategic threat. But that could change: the further development and profusion of smaller, low-tech nuclear devices and of chemical and biological weapons will make obscure "freedom fighters" strategic menaces. An economy-of-scale is no longer necessary to produce weapons of mass destruction. The United States cannot sustain its monopoly over new military technologies, many of which are not expensive and can be acquired by our adversaries through free trade. While the average engagement during the Civil War featured 26,000 men per square mile of battlefront, the figure is now 240, and it will dwindle further as war becomes increasingly unconventional and less dependent on manpower.

Our responses to the outrages of these warriors are inconceivable without the element of surprise, making democratic consultation an afterthought.

War is subject to democratic control only when it is a condition distinctly separate from peace. In Cold War confrontations such as Korea and Vietnam popular opinion played a major role, but a protracted state of quasi-conflict marked by commando raids and electronic strikes on enemy computer systems—in which the swiftness of our reaction is the "killer variable"—will not be guided by public opinion to the same extent.[8] Such conflict will feature warriors on one side, motivated by grievance and rapine, and an aristocracy of statesmen, military officers, and technocrats on the other, motivated, one hopes, by ancient virtue.

We may, of course, face military conflicts not only with warrior groups, but also with great powers such as China. But rather than deploy its soldiers against ours, so as to play by our rules, an adversary may prefer to use computer viruses against us, or unleash its warrior-allies from the Middle East, supplied with its military technology, even while it denies any connection with such stateless terrorists. Russia, too, could make strategic use of terrorists and international criminals in order to fight an undeclared war. Precisely because we are militarily superior to any group or nation, we should expect to be attacked at our weakest points, beyond the boundaries of international law.

Vigilance demands that we remember the Trojans of Homer's *Iliad*. They were the envy of the world: urbane and civilized, surrounded by magnificent buildings and farmlands, wanting only to be left alone, and believing that their wealth and success could always buy a solution. Yet they were besieged by piratical chieftains from across the water, who were driven to war by the Greek gods—gods who, with their intrigues and temper tantrums, are timeless reflections of human irrationality. "Three thousand years have not changed the human condition," observes the classicist Bernard Knox, "we are still lovers and victims of the will to violence. . . ."[9]

Writing in 1939, as her native France was about to be overrun by Nazis, the philosopher and resistance activist Simone Weil celebrated *The Iliad* as the "purest mirror" of our collective experience; it showed how "force, today as in the past, is at the center of all human history. . . ."[10]

The United States is a peaceful, commercial republic that has usually tried to eschew war. But its leaders should be able to appreciate Homer's description of the defenders of Troy, awaiting their dawn attack on the Greeks:

> And so their spirits soared
> as they took positions down the passageways of battle
> all night long, and the watchfires blazed among them.
> Hundreds strong, as stars in the night sky glittering
> round the moon's brilliance blaze in all their glory . . .[11]

In one respect at least, ancient war was more civilized than our own. The aim of ancient war was generally to kill or capture the opposing chief and display him in a cage. Because of the primitive state of technology, the only way to get to the opposing leader and his inner circle was to cut through the mass of his people and army, necessitating bloody battles and great cruelty. But since the Enlightenment, Western leaders have exempted themselves from retribution and have sought to punish each other indirectly: by destroying each other's armies and—since Grant and Sherman—by making the civilian populations suffer as well. But is it really more honorable to kill thousands by high-altitude bombing than by the sword and ax? In Kosovo, our air attacks were far more effective against civilian targets than military ones. Yet, impending precision-guidance technologies—in which bullets can be directed to specific targets like warheads—will make strikes on the offending chief quite practical. In the future, satellites may track the movements of specific individuals through their neuro-biological signatures the way that CAT scans do now from a few inches away. We will reinvent ancient war; it will soon be possible to kill or capture the perpetrators of great cruelties rather than harm their subject populations, which in many cases are also their victims.[12]

Would it have been more humane to assassinate Milosevic and his inner circle rather than bomb Serbia for ten weeks? In the future, such assassinations will be possible. Because many of our future enemies may not inhabit a country as technologically developed as Serbia, there may be no suitable targets like electrical and water-treatment plants to bomb. The only target may be the offending chief or warrior himself. In eastern Afghanistan, where Osama bin Laden hides out, attacking his "infrastructure" means destroying only a few burlap tents, cell phones, and computers, all of which are immediately replaceable.[13]

Because future war will feature precision attacks on command posts, hitting those computer nerve centers will often mean killing the political leadership. Either the law against assassinations that sprang from our Vietnam experience will be scrapped, or it will be sidestepped.[14]

Whether or not future wars are bloodless, there will be an undeniable ancientness to the way in which we conduct them. Kosovo, from our point of view, was a bloodless war: thousands of civilians (mostly Kosovar Albanians) died, so that there would be no NATO casualties. But had a dozen NATO planes been shot down, Clinton might have been forced to call off the war. Our appetite for war is similar to the Romans', whose professional and salaried legions had no desire to fight warriors eager for glorious death. Thus, the Romans avoided open field engagements in favor of expensive and systematic sieges in which their own casualties were minimized.[15] The Romans were also protected beneath cumbersome helmets, breastplates, shoulder guards, and foot greaves, even though this reduced their agility. We are not the first great empire to despise casualties.

"If military action is cost-free," Michael Ignatieff asks, "what democratic restraints will remain on the resort to force?"[16] It is only the specter of casualties that engages the public, sparking a debate that has democratic significance because it reaches beyond the media and intellectual communities. When I was in New Mexico and Colorado at the start of the Kosovo air war, I noticed that televisions everywhere I went were tuned to entertainments, especially game shows, not to CNN's continuous war coverage. The United States could bomb anyplace in the world for weeks, I thought, and the public might not object, provided that there were no American casualties and the stock market was not adversely affected.

Left to themselves, most leaders in the post–Cold War West would avoid all nonstrategic interventions with the risks that they carry, if not for the media and intellectual communities. Because the elite media is dominated by cosmopolitans who inhabit the wider world beyond the nation-state, it has a tendency to emphasize universal moral principles over national self-interest. "Most newsmen," says Walter Cronkite, "feel very little allegiance to the established order. I think they are inclined to side with humanity rather than with authority and institutions."[17] In the hands of the media, the language of human rights—the highest level of altruism—becomes a powerful weapon that can lead us into wars that perhaps we should not fight.[18]

When the media finds a cause it can rally around, it can both shape and replace public opinion, as it did in Bosnia and Kosovo, when the media was overwhelmingly interventionist while the public, as the polls showed, remained unenthusiastic. The media and intellectual communities are professional castes no less distinguishable than those of military officers, doctors, insurance agents, and so on—and no more representative of the American population. As with other professional groups, they are often more influenced by each other than by those outside their social network. Faced with an indifferent public, this quasi-aristocracy may shape the views of Western leaders much as the ancient nobles did of their emperors. And the media's arguments will be difficult to resist. Human rights arguments advanced by the media at their most extreme have a distinctly inquisitional air.

Television correspondents at the scene of catastrophes, like the Israeli bombing of Beirut in 1982 and starvation in Somalia a decade later, manifest an impassioned tunnel vision in which sheer emotion replaces analysis: nothing matters to them except the horrendous spectacle before their eyes—*about which something must be done!* The media embodies classical liberal values, which concern themselves with individuals and their well-being, whereas foreign policy is often concerned with the relationships between states and other large groups. Thus, the media is more likely to be militaristic when individual rights and suffering are concerned, rather than when a state's vital interests are threatened.

Of course, there may be times when the undisciplined emotions of correspondents and human rights activists are exactly what leaders need to hear, as in Sarajevo in 1992 and 1993. Statesmanship is about distinguishing between what is just and what is merely sanctimonious, or impractical. A wise and hesitant determinism will always require triage.

"The side that knows when to fight and when not to will take the victory," says Sun-Tzu. "There are roadways not to be traveled, armies not to be attacked, walled cities not to be assaulted."[19] Indeed, the increasing tendency for urban warfare—Tuzla, Mogadishu, Karachi, Panama City, Beirut, Gaza, and so on—as well as interventions in anarchic territories like Somalia and Sierra Leone, may compel a ruthlessness on our part that the very people demanding intervention cannot bear. As the Athenian general Nicias said, warning in 415 B.C. against intervention in Sicily:

> We must not disguise from ourselves that we go to found a city among strangers and enemies, and that he who undertakes such an enterprise should be prepared to become master of the country the first day he lands, or failing in this to find everything hostile to him.[20]

As Americans were in Vietnam, the Athenians had been lured into Sicily by their allies. Fearing the domino effect of growing Syracusan power, the Athenians came to believe that the conquest of far-off Sicily was crucial to the maintenance of their empire.

Prosperity had made the Athenians arrogant about their chances of success and too fervid about their cause. Because they underestimated the great effort and the brutality that would be required to prevail, the expedition ended in tragedy.

Prudence dictates that we approach casualty-free war as a myth, despite technological advances such as bullets that incapacitate without injuring. War is uncertainty, characterized by friction, chance, and disorder, as Clausewitz says. According to Marine Lieutenant General Paul Van Riper, American forces will have to operate in a range of settings, "from deserts to foliage, to densely populated urban areas with embedded antagonists"—environments not conducive to technological dominance.[21] Laser and electro-optically guided munitions will not track targets through heavy tree cover, and will not preclude civilian casualties in cities. Even when they work well, computer-operated sensors and listening devices may swamp military organizations with undigestible data. As more information accumulates, the difference between information and real knowledge could widen. Robert McNamara's predictive universe, with its quantitative measurements and game theory assumptions, led us deeper into the mire of Vietnam. Exclusive reliance on technology, at once naïve and arrogant, takes little account of local history, traditions, terrain, and other factors that are essential for making wise judgments.

Luckily for the Clinton administration, the sophisticated Serbs of Belgrade were not North Vietnamese; they were ready to give up after our bombs disrupted their water supplies. Perhaps we in the West would also admit defeat if an enemy stopped our running water, our phones, and our electricity. But we should not expect warriors with very few material possessions at risk to be so fragile.

Bullets that don't kill and sonic waves that immobilize a crowd by causing a sensation of nausea and diarrhea may facilitate an individual commando operation, but warriors will interpret such an aversion to violence as weakness, emboldening their cause.

"Future war may become *more* savage, not less so," writes Air Force Colonel Charles Dunlap Jr. "An adversary waging neo-absolutist war could resort to a variety of horrific actions . . . of a low-tech variety to offset and divert high-tech U.S. forces."[22] The enemy will take hostages and place critical supplies susceptible to our precision bombing beneath schools and hospitals. For such adversaries, our moral values—our fear of collateral damage—represent our worst vulnerabilities. The most sincere and heart-breaking truth of the ancients is the vast gulf that separates political-military virtue from individual moral perfection. It is such a truth that may help define the twenty-first century, as we are forced to choose in the midst of high-tech war between what is right and what is unfortunately necessary.

Another problem, according to Colonel Dunlap, will be the unwitting collusion between the global media and our enemies. Dunlap and other defense analysts envision massive, "vertically integrated" media conglomerates with their own surveillance satellites. One firm, Aerobureau of McLean, Virginia, can already deploy a flying newsroom: an aircraft equipped with multiple satellite video, audio, and data links, gyro-stabilized cameras, and the ability to operate camera-equipped vehicles on earth by remote control. Dunlap asks, "[W]hat need will there be for our future enemies to spend money building extensive intelligence capabilities? The media will become the 'poor man's intelligence service.'"

The media is no longer simply the fourth estate, without which the other three branches of government could not operate honestly and effectively. Because of technology and the consolidation of news organizations—similar to the consolidation of airline and automobile alliances—the media is becoming a world power in its own right. The power of the media is willful and dangerous because it dramatically affects Western policy while bearing no responsibility for the outcome. Indeed, the media's moral perfectionism is possible only because it is politically unaccountable.

When America became an independent nation, the press was meant to keep government honest. Alerting the public to humanitarian problems overseas is germane to that role; directing policy is not, particularly if officials are forced to operate at a lower level of altruism than the media. A statesman's primary responsibility is to his country, while the media thinks in universal terms. Emotional coverage of Somalia by a world media foreshadowed an American intervention that, because it was ill-defined, led to the worst disaster for U.S. troops since Vietnam—a disaster that helped influence policymakers against intervention in Rwanda. In a world of constant crises, policymakers must be very selective about where and when they believe it worthwhile to get engulfed in the Clausewitzian "uncertainty" of conflict.

Just as future wars will, in many ways, be ancient, so will the nature of military alliances and the reasons we go to war in the first place. If Europeans ever deploy a military force that is truly independent of the United States, that may only lead to the U.S. moving closer to Russia and other powers in order to counter it. Thus a future European army can only be quasi-independent of NATO. As in *The*

Peloponnesian War, a world of shifting alliances will once again demonstrate the language of power balancing.

The notion of "just war," advanced by Hugo Grotius, echoed Saint Augustine and the medieval theologians, who sought to define circumstances under which Christendom could rightfully give battle. Grotius's "just war" presupposed the existence of a Leviathan—the pope or the Holy Roman emperor—to enforce a moral code. But in a world without a universal arbiter of justice, discussions of war as "just" or "unjust" carry little meaning beyond the intellectual and legal circles in which such discussions take place. States and other entities—whether the United States or the Tamil Tigers—will go to war when they decide it is in their interests (strategic, moral, or both) and will, consequently, be unconcerned if others view their aggression as unjust. According to polls, more than 90 percent of voting-age Greeks—citizens of a NATO democracy—thought our air campaign against Serbia "unjust." But we ignored the Greek public's interpretation of "just war" and did what we felt was right and necessary. The Greek public was using what it thought was a moral argument to justify a national interest: the Serbs were fellow Orthodox Christians and historic allies of the Greeks. However, that is what all nations do in wartime; it isn't only the Greeks.

Ho Chi Minh killed at least 10,000 of his own civilians prior to the entry of American troops into Vietnam. Did this make our intervention in Vietnam just? Perhaps, but it was still a mistake. The Mexican War was probably unjust—motivated as it was by sheer territorial aggression. But it was a war worth fighting: the United States acquired Texas and the entire Southwest, including California.

In the twenty-first century, as in the nineteenth, we will initiate hostilities—whether in the form of Special Forces operations or computer viruses directed at enemy command centers—whenever it is absolutely necessary and we see a clear advantage in doing so, and we will justify it morally after the fact. Nor is that cynical. The moral basis of our foreign policy will depend upon the character of our nation and its leaders, not upon the absolutes of international law.

Nevertheless, there is a model that explains how states and other groups are likely to approach war in the future. It is an age-old model based on an ancient code of honor, explained in an essay by Michael Lind.[23] Lind says that in primitive societies, lawless frontier towns, and the world of organized crime, injustice has always been redressed by the injured themselves, or by their powerful protectors; thus, the safety of the weak rests upon the willingness of their protectors to wield power. Indeed, feudal relationships between stronger and weaker states have marked world politics since time immemorial. Even today, civilian economic powers like Germany and Japan and niche states like oil-rich Kuwait and trading tiger Singapore have specific functions in a Western world order, in which the United States provides military security.

In places where the rule of law does prevail, one is expected to suffer insults without resorting to violence. But in a lawless society, a willingness to suffer insults indicates weakness that, in turn, may invite attack. A world without a Leviathan is somewhat similar: an alliance leader must play the role of barbarian chieftain. In theory, international law governs world politics; in practice, relations between great powers are regulated by a sort of *Code Duello.* Lind notes that "Khrushchev's conception of 'peaceful coexistence' and Third World competition, and the establishment of a Hot Line, were designed to ritualize the struggle for power, not to end it." Such conventions, he continues, "might be compared to the elaborate rules surrounding the aristocratic duel." Such a code may not be Judeo-Christian, yet it is moral just the same. Even in a lawless realm, too extreme a response—killing thousands of civilians in Beirut for the sake of protecting its northern border, as Israel did in 1982—may be perceived as wanton violence, and thus lack legitimacy. In any age, a reputation for power must be balanced by one for mercy. A barbarian chieftain may occasionally have to defend immoral clients (like U.S. support for some dictators during the Cold War), but if he does so too often to the exclusion of all else, his chieftaincy may lose respect and consequently be toppled. A future in which rival chiefs risk assassination as never before—with surprise attacks on computer command posts—is one perfectly suited for a *Code Duello*.

Systems in which two great powers confront each other in a ritualized struggle, as in the Cold War, tend to be more stable than the present one, in which there are many secondary powers while the primary power is still not a Leviathan.[24] In pre–twentieth-century Europe, when one state became too powerful, others often came together to balance it. But there is also the opposite tendency: for weak states to appease a rising power, as when many Third World states aligned themselves with the Soviet Union at the height of its strength in the 1960s and the 1970s. That is happening now, as the ex-Communist and developing worlds seek to emulate America's model of democratic capitalism. But we should never forget that such a positive development rests upon our power as a chieftain. Romania and Bulgaria copied fascism when Nazi Germany was ascendant. Now that America is ascendant, they copy our democracy.

If we are weak militarily—if we aren't able to meet the rising challenge of warriors—our political values may be eclipsed worldwide.

Bernard Knox writes that according to the early Greeks, the past and present, because they are visible, are "in front of us," while the future, "invisible, is behind us. . . ."[25] The future of warfare is already behind us, in ancient times. And so, as we shall see, is the future of global governance.

CHAPTER X

WARRING STATES

CHINA AND GLOBAL

GOVERNANCE

Since the collapse of the Berlin Wall in 1989 an array of theories has been advanced regarding the global political future. Behind the optimistic theories lies the implicit assumption that prosperous and rational-minded elites are sufficiently dominant to lead the world toward more democracy, human rights, and economic integration. The pessimistic theories that foresee dysfunctional democracies, cultural clashes, and anarchy call attention to the weakness of these elites, particularly their inability to control a swarm of willful and irrational actors, embittered often by underdevelopment.

Social theories tend to be linear. They describe a series of incidents and processes leading toward some definable end. But the world is characterized by simultaneity: many different kinds of incidents and processes happening at the same time leading toward different ends. Thus at best, a social theory is a useful failure; rather than prove its point, it gives people a new perspective on events, making them see the familiar in an unfamiliar light. Because all of these theories—optimistic and pessimistic—capture some important trend in a world going in different directions at once, they can be synthesized into a composite global picture that for all its complexity and contradictions has a concrete theme. An example of a similarly complex and contradictory world that can still be made sense of is found in Book Eight of *The Peloponnesian War.*

Thucydides did not bring his story to a proper conclusion at his death in northern Greece around 400 B.C., but he may have stopped writing before that. The sheer complexity of political and military developments in the Greek archipelago may have become too much of a burden for him.[1]

Book Eight, the final book of *The Peloponnesian War,* has only a thin story line. Following the military disaster in Sicily in which the Athenians had overextended themselves, they nonetheless surprised their adversaries by building more ships and continuing the war against Sparta. In a series of naval battles, the Athenians were victorious. On the eastern Aegean island of Samos, the Athenians supported a revolt against the pro-Spartan oligarchy that brought Samos into an alliance with Athens. But on another eastern island, Chios, local factions helped by Sparta successfully revolted against Athens. Meanwhile, Sparta and Persia entered into a treaty that helped Sparta capture additional islands. Yet Persia was at the same time negotiating with Athens. On the home front, Athens was divided between pro-democratic and pro-oligarchic forces, the latter friendly to Sparta. Sparta's allies, the Persians, were also divided because of the rivalry between their two senior commanders, Pharnabazus in the northern Aegean and Tissaphernes in the south. But the rivalry between the two Persian commanders did less harm to Persia than the political divide in Athens did to that city-state.

Although Thucydides does not complete the story, a loose and tenuous theme begins to emerge through this seesawing complexity: the hollow victory of Sparta, which cannot maintain its newfound hegemony over the Greek archipelago without the help of Persia. Thus, Sparta ends up guarding the western flank of Persia's own fragile and chaotic empire.[2]

A similarly loose and tenuous theme emerges by combining all the post–Cold War theories. Here is one scenario:

Liberal democracy conquers the former Warsaw Pact nations, with Russia and one or two Balkan states the exceptions. It also conquers the southern cone of Latin America, much of the Far East, and a few other places. In much of the developing world, though, democracy exists more in name than in fact, often taking the form of "hybrid" regimes. Mexico holds successful elections, but has difficulty building institutions such as police and reliable law courts; the result is barely manageable turmoil. India remains officially a "democratic success story," but only if one avoids the ground-level reality of urban gangs, fixed local elections, the growing scarcity of water, and vigilante justice. Both India and Mexico are undermined by a volcano of unemployed youth in urban slums that results in the formation of volatile populist movements; nevertheless, both these flawed democracies survive and generate high-tech industries. Indonesia, Pakistan, Nigeria, and other countries are not so lucky, though what emerges there is not headline-grabbing, Somalia-style breakdowns but simply a higher degree of chronic unrest than in India and Mexico. Cultural and civilizational stresses, as well as demographic and environmental ones, are everywhere apparent.

Meanwhile, in China, pressure from an expanding urban middle class leads to more democracy; the result is violence and ethnic separatism, aggravated by resource scarcity. Nevertheless, globalization is triumphant, even though it is compromised by frequent, violent backlashes generated by populist movements throughout the developing world. On the other hand, wealthy high-tech metroplexes dominated by global corporations, and with their own foreign trade policies, characterize southeastern China, Singapore, the Mekong River, the Pacific Northwest, Catalonia, and other locales.[3] Places such as Greater Beirut, Greater São Paulo, and Bangalore in India are vibrant city-states, but troubled by armies of poor people. As the power of both corporations and slum dwellers increases, that of the traditional state declines. But in Russia, China, India, Pakistan, and elsewhere, the state fights back with irresponsible policies and weapons programs.

Within the United States, the most troublesome issue is not an economic crash following years of unparalleled prosperity, but tensions with Mexico that prosperity and democratization unleash. Mexico becomes increasingly democratic, but remains lawless and poverty-stricken. Because of Mexico's democracy, the United States is forced to treat it as an equal, even as Mexico's elected government, prodded by populist pressures, makes demands that the United States cannot satisfy. These two vastly unequal societies integrate at breakneck speed; the result is social upheaval on both sides of the border that is positive in the long term but marked by crises in the short term. The traumas of a unifying world, good and bad, creative and destructive—including democratization and clashes of civilization—are funneled through the tumultuous historic consolidation of Mexico and the United States.

In sub-Saharan Africa, along with parts of the Middle East and South Asia—with the world's most dramatic population growth rates through 2050—violent conflict shapes events the way it did in Europe in the twentieth century.[4] Nevertheless, the profusion of anarchy in the developing world puts pressure on global elites to strengthen and enlarge international institutions. World *governance* becomes a reality, but that does not lead to a world government. The Leviathan that emerges through the fog of all the wars and chaos and sealed-off zones of prosperity is fragile and incomplete. Nevertheless, it is something that has never existed before.

The twenty-first century turns out to be nearly as violent as the twentieth. Because of the withering of nation-states, the rise of city-states, and many overlapping and informal sovereignties, a benign feudalism reigns. Yet, because more and better global institutions increase the scope for punishment of the Unjust, the gap narrows between morality at home and morality in foreign affairs. It is a world no less and no more united than Persia's ancient empire. The closer we look at antiquity, the more we learn about this new world.

The Sumerian city-states of the third millennium B.C. in Mesopotamia, the early Mauryan empire of the fourth century B.C. in India, and the early Han empire of the second century B.C. in China are all examples of political systems in which diverse and far-flung territories were sufficiently involved with each other, through trade and political alliances, to regulate their behavior and allow for similar moral standards.[5] Rather than *raison d'état*, there was an equivalent *raison de système*—the belief that making the system work constituted the highest morality, because the alternative was chaos. Fear of violent death, as Hobbes would later tell us, made men give up part of their freedom for the sake of order, which led to an often weak and shadowy imperialism.

Ancient Sumer, unlike pharaonic Egypt, was not a single empire but an assemblage of at least twelve independent walled cities in southern Mesopotamia, near the Persian Gulf: Ur, Kish, Erech, Nippur, Lagash, and so on, each with its own personality, commercial life, ruling god, and strategic interests. Yet they were all united by a common culture and language. Inevitable disputes arose over land, water, and the regulation of commerce. The solution was neither absolutism as in Egypt nor the complete independence that characterized relations between the Sumerians and their non-Sumerian neighbors; rather, a system emerged that could be called hegemony. One city-state, by virtue of its power, would mediate the disputes of the others, until its own power was eclipsed by one of its neighbors, which then succeeded it as hegemon. From 2800 B.C. to 2500 B.C., the city-states of Kish, Erech, Ur, and Lagash vied for ascendancy. Although the competition eventually weakened Sumer (which was later conquered by neighboring Elam and Akkad) it was, nevertheless, a workable system that preserved unity while permitting each city-state a significant degree of sovereignty.

Fourth-century B.C. India, by contrast, was a more complex patchwork of communities. Many of these, while independent, were united by a common Hinduism and constrained by a mesh of rules that had arisen from trade and political contacts with each other. Because the survival of each city-state depended upon its relations with surrounding states, here, too, *raison de système* constituted the highest political morality. Obviously, strong states tried to dominate weaker ones, but even when successful, they did not interfere with the daily commerce and customs of their vassals. Yet, unlike Sumer, there was no hegemon and thus politics was more chaotic. That situation changed when Chandragupta Maurya founded an empire in 321 B.C. based in northeastern India, which would extend throughout much of the Asian subcontinent and rely upon Greek and Persian imperial practices.

Chandragupta's chief advisor was one Kautilya, the author of a political classic, the *Arthashastra* ("Book of the State"). Kautilya's book has been compared to Machiavelli's *Prince* because of its keen, albeit ruthless, insight into human nature. Like Machiavelli, Kautilya shows how a prince, whom he calls "the conqueror," can create an empire by exploiting the relationships between various city-states. He says that any city-state that touches one's own should be considered an enemy, because it will have to be subdued in the course of building an empire. But a distant city-state that borders an enemy should be considered a friend, because it can be used against the enemy without threatening one's own security. That same concept made Nixon and Kissinger see Mao's China as a friend in the early 1970s, because it bordered our enemy, the Soviet Union, and was threatened by it.[6] Kautilya's advice is virtuous because, as he says, the aim of conquest is the happiness of each city-state through the creation of stability. Conquered territories, he writes, should be governed as they had been before, their way of life preserved, and rather than exact tribute, taxes should be returned to the conquered as compensation for their subjugation.

The empire established by Chandragupta, with the help of Kautilya, guaranteed security over an extraordinarily large area in which trade flourished. It was an area that because of the slowness of land and sea travel was, like Greece during the Peloponnesian War, equivalent to today's entire world.

But the most intriguing case of an ancient system of governance that allowed the territories within it to be at once independent and interdependent is China. While Greece, Sumer, India, and other Near Eastern civilizations were all influenced and affected by other empires (particularly Persia), China was a universe unto itself, its primitive nomadic neighbors drawn into its orbit.

From the late twelfth to the early eighth century B.C., central China was a feudal system loosely governed by the Zhou royal house, based along the Wei River. The Zhou suzerain ruled indirectly through as many as 1,770 fiefdoms, each governed by a garrison commander or a member of the extended royal family. In 770 B.C., the Zhou capital, weakened by power struggles, was sacked by barbarians. The feudal system survived, though the fiefdoms became increasingly independent.

Gradually, a number of strong states emerged, especially Ch'u in the south and Chin in the northwest. Somewhat weaker than these, yet still strong enough to command their own mini-empires, were Ch'in (Qin) and Ch'i in the east. Thus, in the sixth century B.C., a balance of power reigned among Ch'u, Chin, Ch'in, and Ch'i. There was also an antihegemonical league of states to check the rising influence of Ch'u, and middle powers such as Zheng.[7] Zheng, with a vigilant government and a strong military, switched alliances fourteen times between Ch'u and the anti-Ch'u league, in order to improve its position. Yet, because each power required alliances with other ones, a system of sorts emerged, encouraging China's military and political integration. This process was helped by trade, the growth of cities, and the replacement of feudal structures with a somewhat standardized bureaucracy.

In the fifth century B.C., Ch'u was again challenged, this time by its southern neighbors, Wu and Yueh, with Yueh emerging victorious. Meanwhile, the great powers of Chin, Ch'in, and Ch'i all declined because of internal power struggles. The complexity of Chinese politics intensified further. After a half-century of disorder, seven major powers and six minor ones arose. The only old kingdom to survive the shakeout was Ch'u, which, though a southern power, had assimilated the northern culture of its rivals—part of the process of integration that was sweeping China despite the political fractures.

What followed next (from 475 B.C. to 221 B.C.) was yet another cycle of power struggles known as the *Chan-kuo*, the period of the "Warring States." It was a progressive disharmony; many of the cultural patterns and bureaucratic structures that were to characterize China for the next two millennia developed during the Warring States period. The era also produced great philosophy, including that of Sun-Tzu, author of *The Art of Warfare*, and the unrelated Hsun-tzu, a Confucian thinker whose most famous maxim is: "[M]an's nature is evil; his goodness is only acquired through training." It is something that Hobbes or Hamilton might have written.

The cultural and bureaucratic consolidation of China during the Warring States period led to the number of great powers being reduced from seven to three by the middle of the third century B.C. There was Ch'u in the south, Ch'in in the west, and Ch'i in the east, the last two re-emerging from long periods of internal strife. By 223 B.C., Ch'in (Qin) had subdued its two rivals and established the first unified empire in Chinese history. In 206 B.C., a revolt replaced Ch'in's short-lived dynasty with that of the Han, which lasted for over four hundred years—the first great pan-Chinese empire.

The Han empire was no monochromic dictatorship ruled exclusively from an imperial capital. Rather, it represented a grand harmony of diverse peoples and systems—kingships, warlordships, and so on. Despite all their power struggles the individual Warring States had evolved through centuries of cultural and bureaucratic consolidation into the diverse elements of a system greater than themselves. If one looks at ancient China as a microcosm of the whole world, then the twenty-first century may witness the rough equivalent of the early Han empire: a global system emerging out of the great conflicts and anarchy of the Warring States period.

In *The Evolution of International Society,* a British former diplomat, Adam Watson, notes sagely that political integration in ancient Greece, Sumer, India, and China always required common cultural assumptions to mold rules and institutions.[8] While today's world is culturally diverse, a singular, upper-middle-class cosmopolitan culture is forming, nevertheless. As this nouvelle cuisine culture expands, so will international institutions. Just as modern states arose contemporaneously with an industrial middle class, the expansion of this new global upper class will ultimately mark the transcendence of states themselves.

And just as the most powerful states in the twentieth century each had its own economy of scale to service the needs of its population, the highly particularized needs of the new global cosmopolitans will require a worldwide economy of scale in which states and regions may specialize in one range of products or another. In such a way, humanity might close a rift in the historical cycle, by re-establishing on a planetary basis the ancient systems of Greece, Sumer, India, and China.

I am not saying, pace Marx, that there is a rigid direction to history; nor am I saying that history *is just one damned thing after another*. I am merely suggesting, as did Montesquieu in the eighteenth century, that things seem to be moving in a certain, albeit vague, direction toward a "minimal international morality," and that some large patterns are discernible.[9]

The emergence of some kind of loose world governance is probably inevitable—barring a major war between two or more great powers such as the United States and China. Continuing chaos in sub-Saharan Africa and elsewhere may transpire independently of the convergence of elite global institutions while impelling it at the same time. Every new African war will generate more international meetings in places like Geneva and Washington that will increase the will of the participants to respond better the next time. In such a way, international organizations and multinational rescue squads will continue to evolve and mature. Great powers such as the United States will delegate responsibility to international bodies so as not to overburden themselves; it will be done in the name of a universal morality for the sake of a national self-interest.

But the probability of global political convergence says little about its usefulness. The European Union (EU) is a system. But it is still unclear whether the EU will be effective or simply foster a vapid, bureaucratic despotism that becomes a breeding ground for nasty nationalist reactions. In the third century B.C., the Ch'in (Qin) emperor united China for the first time ever, but his adoption of legalism—a doctrine advocating inflexible bureaucratic regimentation—led to the dynasty's collapse after less than two decades. Conversely, the Han dynasty that followed lasted over four hundred years because it mixed the best of legalism with Confucianism, which taught tradition and moderation. Whether it is an inspiring EU or a somewhat despotic and cowardly one, whether it is unity through the oppressive legalism of the Ch'in emperors or through the more progressive Confucianism of the Han emperors, whether a global system reflects the values of the Western democracies or does not, makes all the difference in the world.

Remember that the unity of Greece which came about with the conclusion of the Peloponnesian War did not necessarily advance civilization, for it meant the defeat of Athens's democracy at the hands of Sparta and its ally, Persia. But the subsuming of the Warring States under the Confucian value system of the Han emperors was a good thing; its global equivalent can now only be achieved by the United States.

The late English political philosopher E. H. Carr writes, "To internationalize government in any real sense means to internationalize power. . . ."[10] Power cannot be created out of thin air. The creation of the United Nations in 1945 did not make it powerful, or even useful. Though in its sixth decade, the U.N. is effective to the degree that it has the tacit approval of a great power, especially the United States. When the U.N. does truly act alone, that is because no great power sees it in its interest to intervene in the matter. Likewise, the exalted new status of international institutions—the war crimes tribunal in The Hague, for example—would be impossible were it not for the military and political victory of the Western allies in the Cold War, which rid international bodies of Soviet leverage. Global institutions like the war crimes tribunal are an outgrowth of Western power, not a replacement for it.

"Historically," writes Carr, "every approach in the past to a world society has been the product of the ascendancy of a single Power."[11] There is no sign that this has changed. Globalization means the spread of American business practices, adopted by each culture to its own needs: some good, some bad. The ascendancy of that model—along with that of democracy, war crimes tribunals, and effective peacekeeping organizations—required a decades-long struggle against the Soviet Union that entailed vast covert operations and nuclear weapons systems, which could not always be explained or justified in terms of a universal morality.

And for American power to endure, it will need to be impelled by a more primitive level of altruism than that of the universal society it seeks to encourage. American patriotism—honoring the flag, July Fourth celebrations, and so on—must survive long enough to provide the military armature for an emerging global civilization that may eventually make such patriotism obsolete. Greater individual freedom and more democracy may be the outcomes of a universal society, but its creation cannot be wholly democratic. After all, two hundred–odd states, in addition to hundreds of influential nonstate forces, mean a plethora of narrow interests that cannot advance any wider interest without the organizing mechanism of a great hegemon.[12]

Alas, our prize for winning the Cold War is not merely the opportunity to expand NATO, or to hold democratic elections in places that never had them, but something far broader: *We and no-*

body else will write the terms for international society. As Joseph Conrad told a friend during World War I, it is not specifically for parliamentary democracy that we fought, but "for freedom of thought and development in whatever form."[13]

Churchill's most sublime realization may have been that Britain was near sunset, and another stronger and rising power that shared its values was poised to take its place: the United States of America. Churchill saw in Franklin Roosevelt what Chamberlain did not: the great politician with whom he would trump Hitler, afterward allowing Britain to recede gracefully from history. But the United States lacks that luxury. There is no credible force on the horizon with both our power and our values. The United Nations or a combination of international organizations may one day become that force. But that is by no means certain. Kant's essay on "Perpetual Peace" envisions an assemblage of freedom-loving nations; not a universal organization. Thus, for the United States, the most important decades in foreign policy lie ahead.

A century of disastrous utopian hopes has brought us back to imperialism, that most ordinary and dependable form of protection for ethnic minorities and others under violent assault: whether Jews protected by the sultan of Turkey from the bloodthirstiness of local ethnic majorities; or Moslems in Bosnia protected tardily by the imperial legions of the West. Despite our anti-imperial traditions, and despite the fact that imperialism is delegitimized in public discourse, an imperial reality already dominates our foreign policy. What are the NATO missions in Bosnia and Kosovo other than imperial protectorates, with which the Romans and Habsburgs would have been familiar? The right-wing gadfly Patrick Buchanan is wrong to say that America is a republic, not an empire; it is most certainly both.

The very weakness and flexibility of such a nontraditional American-led empire will constitute its strength. The power of this new imperium will derive from it never having to be declared, saving it from the self-delusive, ceremonial trappings of the United Nations. Joseph Nye Jr., dean of Harvard's Kennedy School, speaks of "soft" American hegemony. Sun-Tzu says that the strongest strategic position is "formless"; it is a position that adversaries cannot attack because it exists everywhere and nowhere.[14] An American imperium should be like that. It should function as "a polity on the move," like Xenophon's democratic Greek army, cutting through the farthest reaches of the chaotic Persian empire in 401 B.C., with the troops freely debating over each step.[15]

No other imperial military has been so demonstrably multiethnic, bound by the values of a constitution rather than by blood. Among the MREs (Meals Ready to Eat) consumed by U.S. Special Forces troops are packets labeled halal, suited to the dietary restrictions of Moslems, and kosher for Jews. As I write, the chief of the U.S. Army—one of the Joint Chiefs of Staff—is General Eric Shinseki, a Japanese-American, whose family lived in an internment camp during World War II.

But expanding this multiethnic American imperium can only be done nimbly; a single war with significant loss of American life (for example, in the Taiwan Strait) could ruin the public's appetite for internationalism. Triumphalism has no place in our foreign policy: our ideals will have to grow less rigid and more varied if they are to meet the needs of the far corners of the earth. "Democracy is inimical to imperial mobilization," warns former national security adviser Zbigniew Brzezinski, because of the economic self-denial and human sacrifice that such mobilization entails.[16] Indeed, the restraining power of our own democracy makes it hard for us to demand and orchestrate authentic democratic transitions everywhere. Only through stealth and anxious foresight can America create a secure international system.

CHAPTER XI

TIBERIUS

The larger the scope of our imperium, the more complex our civilization becomes—with its rapidly expanding technical and scientific mandarinate—the more comfortable a statesman must be with loneliness. Because the very size and complexity of our political and military establishments are what make them so vulnerable, our salvation will lie with generalists who are not intimidated by the specialists under their command.

True bravery and independence of thought are best anchored by examples from the past, culled from the pages of the great books. It was the virtuous patriotism Churchill took from those like Livy that helped him maintain the British empire. While our own empire is radically different from Britain's, building a global community will always benefit from such inspiration.

Effective leadership will always reside within the mystery of character. In the 1911 edition of the *Encyclopaedia Britannica*, James Smith Reid, a professor of ancient history at Cambridge

University, wrote the following about the much-maligned Roman emperor of the early first century A.D. Tiberius:

> The penalty of his inscrutability was widespread dislike and suspicion. But behind his defenses there lay an intellect of high power, cold, clear, and penetrating all disguises. Few have ever possessed such mental vision, and he was probably never deceived either about the weaknesses of others or about his own.... Tiberius proved himself capable in every department of the state more by virtue of industry and application than by genius. His mind moved so slowly and he was accustomed to deliberate so long that men sometimes made the mistake of deeming him a waverer. He was in reality one of the most tenacious of men.... The key to much of his character lies in the observation that he had in early life set before himself a certain ideal of what a Roman in high position ought to be, and to this ideal he rigidly adhered.... The care expended by Tiberius on the provinces was unremitting. His favourite maxim was that a good shepherd should shear the flock and not flay it. When he died he left the subject peoples of the empire in a condition of prosperity such as they had never known before and never knew again.[1]

Tiberius left the imperial treasury with twenty times the wealth he had inherited. He abandoned gladiatorial games, and forbade the most outlandish aspects of the imperial cult of personality, such as naming a month after the emperor. The disrepute attached to his name stems mainly from the second part of his rule, when the aged emperor delegated power to the Praetorian Guard, and "developed, under the influence of his fears, a readiness to shed blood."[2] From 23 A.D. until his death in 37 A.D. Tiberius descended into the worst sort of tyrant, building a series of dungeons and torture chambers around his network of villas on the island of Capri where he lived, surrounded by a retinue of guards and sycophants. His cruelty was obscene. Though, it may partially have been the result of mental disease. It is only the first part of his emperorship, from 14 A.D. to 23 A.D., that can be held up as model of capable leadership. Unfortunately, there was no mechanism for a peaceful transfer of power after he had been emperor for nine years.

Still, Tiberius preserved the institutions and imperial boundaries of his predecessor, Augustus, while leaving them sufficiently stable to survive the excesses of his successors like Caligula: "[H]is posture was that of a realist, even a pessimist, without illusions about human destiny, human nature, and politics," writes the contemporary Oxford historian Barbara Levick.[3] He built few cities, annexed few territories, and did not cater to popular whims; rather, he strengthened the territories that Rome already possessed by adding military bases, and combined diplomacy with the threat of force to preserve a peace that was favorable to Rome.[4] "It was in his harsh view of human nature that Tiberius' veneration for the law had its roots," writes Levick. Tiberius realized that in Rome's circumstances, the Senate could be protected only through the overwhelming military power of the emperor. Though, it was the strain of absolute power that ultimately unhinged him, and accounted for his many mistakes and cruelties.[5]

Unlike Churchill or Pericles, Tiberius is not an inspiring role model, but his strengths may be worth examining. In the opinion of many historians, it was because of Tiberius that Rome survived so long in the West. Our future leaders could do worse than be praised for their tenacity, their penetrating intellects, and their ability to bring prosperity to distant parts of the world under America's soft imperial influence. The more successful our foreign policy, the more leverage America will have in the world. Thus, the more likely that future historians will look back on the twenty-first-century United States as an empire as well as a republic, however different from that of Rome and every other empire throughout history. For as the decades and centuries march on, and the United States has had a hundred presidents, or 150 even, instead of forty-three, and they appear in long lists like the rulers of bygone empires—Roman, Byzantine, Ottoman—the comparison with antiquity may grow rather than diminish. Rome, in particular, is a model for hegemonic power, using various means to encourage a modicum of order in a disorderly world—the reason Machiavelli, Montesquieu, and Gibbon devoted so much attention to it.[6] Oliver Wendell Holmes called his fellow Americans "the Romans of the modern world."

One can write endlessly about the differences between the first and twenty-first centuries A.D. But then as now, there is no greater attribute for a ruler than humility built on an accurate assessment of his own limits, from which the finest cunning emerges. Franklin Roosevelt steadily and stealthily moved the United States closer to war with Hitler while at the same time denying it because he knew that an isolationist Congress would not support him. Likewise, Tiberius's campaigns in 5–10 A.D. in Germany and Bohemia made him a chief architect of the Roman imperial system in Europe; yet, when he became emperor, his policy toward that frontier region was one of caution. In 28 A.D., after an ill-considered Roman offensive against barbarians in Lower Germany resulted in heavy Roman loses, Tiberius deliberately hid news of the casualties to avoid coming under popular pressure to avenge them: Tiberius's greatest strength was his awareness of Rome's weaknesses.[7] Under his rule, "the duties of the Roman forces on the borders were confined to watching the peoples on the other side while they destroyed each other." For Rome, such "masterly inactivity achieved tranquility which lasted for a long period."[8] Of course, America cannot be similarly inactive. Nevertheless, the more cautious we are, the more effective we will be.

At the beginning of the twenty-first century, the world media shows little sympathy for the challenges and awful ironies facing those who wield power; it upholds the safer virtue of sympathizing only with the powerless. Yet our greatest presidents knew that the wise employment of force was the surest guide to progress. In the Roosevelt Room of the White House's West Wing, where important staff meetings are held, there is a relief carving of Teddy Roosevelt with these words of the twenty-sixth president—words that might have been written by Machiavelli, Thucydides, or Churchill: "Aggressive fighting for the right is the noblest sport the world affords." Next to that carving, encased in glass, on the mantel of a small fireplace in the room, is the Nobel Peace Prize that Roosevelt won in 1906 for mediating the end of the Russo-Japanese War. Roosevelt had rejoiced at Japan's destruction of the Russian fleet, for he feared Russian influence in Europe. But he wanted Russia weakened rather than destroyed, in order to contain Japan. That was the motive behind his mediation. Power politics in the service of patriotic virtue—a principle as old as the great classical civilizations of China and the Mediterranean—is what that Nobel Peace

Prize in the White House really venerates. To the degree that our Cold War policy was a variant of that outlook, it will never go out of date.

The United States is nothing without its democracy; it is the homeland of freedom rather than of blood.[9] But to deposit judiciously its democratic seeds in a wider world that is closer and more dangerous than ever before, it will be compelled to apply ideals that while not necessarily democratic, are worthy nonetheless. The more respect we have for the truths of the past, the more certain our journey away from it.

SELECTED BIBLIOGRAPHY

Aristotle. *The Politics of Aristotle*. Translated by Peter L. Phillips Simpson. Chapel Hill: University of North Carolina Press, 1997.

Aron, Raymond. *Peace and War: A Theory of International Relations*. Translated by Richard Howard and Annette Baker Fox. Garden City, N.Y.: Doubleday, 1966.

Berlin, Isaiah. *Four Essays on Liberty*. Oxford, Eng.: Oxford University Press, 1969 (essay copyrights 1950 through 1969).

—. *The Proper Study of Mankind: An Anthology of Essays*. Edited by Henry Hardy and Roger Hausheer. Foreword by Noel Annan. New York: Farrar, Straus and Giroux, 1998 (essay copyrights 1949 through 1990).

Bowra, C. Maurice. *The Greek Experience*. New York: World, 1957.

Brzezinski, Zbigniew. *The Grand Chessboard: American Primacy and Its Geostrategic Imperatives*. New York: Basic Books, 1997.

Burckhardt, Jacob. *The Civilization of the Renaissance in Italy*. Translated by S.C.G. Middlemore. New York: Random House [1878] 1954.

Carr, Edward Hallett. *The Twenty Years' Crisis, 1919–1939: An Introduction to the Study of International Relations*. London: Macmillan, 1939.

Chan-kuo Ts'e. Translated and annotated, and with an Introduction by J. I. Crump. Oxford, Eng.: Clarendon, 1970. See also Ian P. McGreal's *Great Literature of the Eastern World*. New York: HarperCollins, 1996.

Churchill, Winston S. *The River War: An Historical Account of the Re-Conquest of the Soudan.* 2 vols. London: Longmans, Green, 1899. Republished by Prion (London, 1997), and in the original two-volume format, with commentary, maps, illustrations, etc., by St. Augustine Press (South Bend, Ind., 2002).

Cicero. *Selected Works.* Translated with an Introduction by Michael Grant. New York: Penguin, 1960.

Clausewitz, Karl von. *On War.* Translated by O. L. Matthijs Jolles. New York: Random House, 1943.

Confucius. *The Analects.* Translated by Raymond Dawson. New York: Oxford University Press, 1993.

Djilas, Milovan. *Wartime.* Translated by Michael B. Petrovich. New York: Harcourt Brace Jovanovich, 1977.

Felix, Christopher. *A Short Course in the Secret War.* New York: Dutton, 1963.

Finer, S. E. *The History of Government from the Earliest Times.* New York: Oxford University Press, 1997.

Flanzbaum, Hilene. *The Americanization of the Holocaust.* Baltimore, Md.: Johns Hopkins University Press, 1999.

Friedrich, Carl J., and Zbigniew K. Brzezinski. *Totalitarian Dictatorship and Autocracy.* Cambridge, Mass.: Harvard University Press, 1956.

Fromkin, David. *Kosovo Crossing: American Ideals Meet Reality on the Balkan Battlefields.* New York: Free Press, 1999.

Gilbert, Martin, and Richard Gott. *The Appeasers.* Boston: Houghton Mifflin, 1963.

Gray, John. *Berlin.* New York: Fontana/HarperCollins, 1995.

———. *Liberalism: Concepts in Social Thought.* Minneapolis: University of Minnesota Press, 1995.

Gress, David. *From Plato to NATO: The Idea of the West and Its Opponents.* New York: Free Press, 1998.

Hamilton, Alexander, James Madison, and John Jay. *The Federalist Papers.* Introduction by Clinton Rossiter. New York: New American Library [1788] 1961.

Handel, Michael I. *Masters of War: Classical Strategic Thought.* London: Frank Cass, 1992.

Herodotus. *The Histories.* Translated by Aubrey de Sélincourt. New York: Penguin, 1954.

Hobbes, Thomas. *Leviathan.* New York: Norton [1651] 1997.

Homer. *The Iliad.* Translated by Robert Fagles. Introduction and notes by Bernard Knox. New York: Penguin, 1990.

Howard, Michael. *The Invention of Peace: Reflections on War and International Order.* New Haven, Conn.: Yale University Press, 2001.

Huntington, Samuel P. *Political Order in Changing Societies.* New Haven, Conn.: Yale University Press, 1968.

————. *The Soldier and the State: The Theory and Politics of Civil-Military Relations.* Cambridge, Mass.: Belknap/Harvard University Press, 1957.

Ibn Khaldu'n. *The Muqaddimah: An Introduction to History.* Translated by Franz Rosenthal. Princeton, N.J.: Bollingen/Princeton University Press, 1958.

Ignatieff, Michael. *Isaiah Berlin: A Life.* New York: Holt, 1998.

————. *Virtual War: Kosovo and Beyond.* New York: Holt, 2000.

Judt, Tony. *The Burden of Responsibility: Blum, Camus, Aron, and the French Twentieth Century.* Chicago: University of Chicago Press, 1998.

Kagan, Donald. *On the Origins of War and the Preservation of Peace.* New York: Doubleday, 1995.

Kagan, Robert. "The Benevolent Empire." *Foreign Policy.* Summer 1998.

Kant, Immanuel. *Groundwork of the Metaphysics of Morals.* Translated by Mary Gregor. Introduction by Christine M. Korsgaard. New York: Cambridge University Press [1785] 1997.

————. *Perpetual Peace and Other Essays on Politics, History, and Morals.* Translated by Ted Humphrey. Indianapolis: Hackett [1784–1795] 1983.

Kapstein, Ethan B., and Michael Mastanduno. *Unipolar Politics: Realism and State Strategies After the Cold War.* New York: Columbia University Press, 1999.

Kennan, George F. *At a Century's Ending: Reflections, 1982–1995.* New York: Norton, 1996.

————. *Realities of American Foreign Policy.* Princeton, N.J.: Princeton University Press, 1954.

Kissinger, Henry. *Diplomacy.* New York: Simon & Schuster, 1994.

————. *Years of Renewal.* New York: Simon & Schuster, 1999.

Landes, David S. *The Wealth and Poverty of Nations.* New York: Norton, 1998.

Ledeen, Michael A. *Machiavelli on Modern Leadership: Why Machiavelli's Iron Rules Are as Timely and Important Today as Five Centuries Ago.* New York: St. Martin's, 1999.

Levick, Barbara. *Tiberius: The Politician.* London: Routledge [1976] 1999.

Lind, Michael. *Vietnam: The Necessary War.* New York: Free Press, 1999.

Livy. *The War with Hannibal:* Books 21–30 of *The History of Rome from Its Foundation.* Translated by Aubrey de Sélincourt. Introduction by Betty Radice. New York: Penguin, 1965.

Luttwak, Edward N. "Toward Post-Heroic Warfare." *Foreign Affairs.* May–June 1995.

McGreal, Ian P. *Great Thinkers of the Western World.* New York: Harper-Collins, 1992.

Machiavelli, Niccolò. *Discourses on Livy.* Translated by Julia Conaway Bondanella and Peter Bondanella. New York: Oxford University Press [1531] 1997.

————. *The Prince.* Translated by Russell Price. Introduction by Quentin Skinner. New York: Cambridge University Press [1532] 1988. See also translation by Angelo Codevilla, New Haven, Conn.: Yale University Press, 1997.

Malthus, Thomas Robert. *An Essay on the Principle of Population.* Edited by Philip Appleman. New York: Norton [1798] 1976.

Manchester, William. *A World Lit Only by Fire: The Medieval Mind and the Renaissance; Portrait of an Age.* Boston: Little, Brown, 1992.

Mansfield, Harvey C. *Machiavelli's Virtue.* Chicago: University of Chicago Press, 1996.

Martinich, A. P. *Thomas Hobbes.* New York: St. Martin's, 1997.

Mathews, Jessica. "Power Shift." *Foreign Affairs.* Jan.–Feb. 1997.

Montesquieu. *The Spirit of the Laws.* Translated and edited by Anne M. Cohler, Basia Carolyn Miller, and Harold Samuel Stone. New York: Cambridge University Press [1748] 1989.

Morgenthau, Hans J. *Politics Among Nations: The Struggle for Power and Peace.* New York: Knopf [1948] 1978.

Murray, Williamson. "Clausewitz Out, Computers In: Military Culture and Technological Hubris." *The National Interest.* Summer 1997.

Niebuhr, Reinhold. *The Irony of American History.* New York: Scribner's, 1952.

Novick, Peter. *The Holocaust in American Life.* Boston: Houghton Mifflin, 1999.

Oakeshott, Michael. *Rationalism in Politics and Other Essays.* Indianapolis: Liberty Fund [1962] 1991.

Ortega y Gasset, José. *The Revolt of the Masses.* Translated by Anthony Kerrigan. South Bend, Ind.: University of Notre Dame Press [1932] 1985.

———. *Toward a Philosophy of History.* New York: Norton, 1941.

Pangle, Thomas L., and Peter J. Ahrensdorf. *Justice Among Nations: On the Moral Basis of Power and Peace.* Lawrence: University Press of Kansas, 1999.

Peters, Ralph. *Fighting for the Future: Will America Triumph?* Mechanicsburg, Pa.: Stackpole, 1999.

Plutarch. *The Lives of the Noble Grecians and Romans.* Vols. 1 and 2. Translated by John Dryden [1683–86]. Edited and revised by Arthur Hugh Clough [1864]. New York: Modern Library, 1992.

Polybius. *The Rise of the Roman Empire.* Translated by Ian Scott-Kilvert. New York: Penguin, 1979.

Qian, Sima. *Records of the Grand Historian: Han Dynasty I and II, Qin Dynasty.* Translated by Burton Watson. New York: Columbia University Press, 1961.

Rahe, Paul A. *Republics Ancient and Modern.* Vol. 1, *The Ancient Regime in Classical Greece.* Vol. 2, *New Modes & Orders in Early Modern Political Thought.* Vol. 3, *Inventions of Prudence: Constituting the American Regime.* Chapel Hill: University of North Carolina Press, 1994.

———. "*The River War:* Nature's Provision, Man's Desire to Prevail, and the Prospects for Peace." In *Churchill as Peacemaker,* edited by James W. Muller. Cambridge, Eng.: Cambridge University Press, 1997.

Sallust. *The Jugurthine War.* Translated by S. A. Handford. New York: Penguin, 1963.

Schlesinger, Arthur M., Jr. *The Cycles of American History.* Boston: Houghton Mifflin, 1986.

Schorske, Carl E. *Thinking with History: Explorations in the Passage to Modernism.* Princeton, N.J.: Princeton University Press, 1998.

Seneca. *Moral and Political Essays.* Edited by John M. Cooper and J. F. Procope. Cambridge, Eng.: Cambridge University Press, 1995.

Smart, J.J.C., and Bernard Williams. *Utilitarianism: For and Against.* Cambridge, Eng.: Cambridge University Press, 1973.

Solzhenitsyn, Aleksandr. *November 1916: The Red Wheel/Knot II.* Translated by H. T. Willetts. New York: Farrar, Straus and Giroux [1984] 1999.

Strassler, Robert B., ed. *The Landmark Thucydides: A Comprehensive Guide to the Peloponnesian War.* New York: Free Press, 1996.

Strauss, Leo. *The Political Philosophy of Hobbes: Its Basis and Its Genesis.* Translated by Elsa M. Sinclair. Chicago: University of Chicago Press [1936, 1952] 1966.

Sun-Tzu. *The Art of Warfare.* Translated by Roger T. Ames. New York: Ballantine, 1993.

Swift, Jonathan. *Gulliver's Travels.* New York: Knopf [1726] 1991.

Tacitus. *The Histories.* Translated by Kenneth Wellesley. New York: Penguin, 1964.

Thucydides. *The Peloponnesian War.* Translated by Thomas Hobbes [1629]. Chicago: University of Chicago Press, 1989.

Toynbee, Arnold J. *A Study of History.* Oxford, Eng.: Oxford University Press, 1946.

Tuchman, Barbara W. *Stilwell and the American Experience in China, 1911–45.* New York: Macmillan, 1970.

Virgil. *The Aeneid.* Translated by Robert Fitzgerald. New York: Random House, 1983.

Waltz, Kenneth. *Man, the State, and War.* New York: Columbia University Press, 1959.

Watson, Adam. *The Evolution of International Society: A Comparative Historical Analysis.* New York: Routledge, 1992.

Weber, Max. *The Profession of Politics.* Plutarch Press [1920] 1989.

Wills, Garry. *Saint Augustine.* New York: Lipper/Viking, 1999.

Yourcenar, Marguerite. *Memoirs of Hadrian.* New York: Farrar, Straus and Giroux [1951] 1963.

Zakaria, Fareed. "Is Realism Finished?" *The National Interest.* Winter 1992–93.

NOTES

PREFACE

1. Richard Francis Burton. *Wanderings in West Africa from Liverpool to Fernando Po* (Mineola, N.Y.: Dover, 1991), pp. 20–21.

CHAPTER 1: THERE IS NO "MODERN" WORLD

1. Mao's nearly three decades in power led to 35 million civilian deaths in China. By comparison, Communist rule in the Soviet Union led to 62 million civilian deaths; Nazi rule in Germany, to 21 million. Rudy J. Rummel, "Statistics of Democide," *The Economist*, Sept. 11, 1999.
2. *Federalist No. 6.*
3. Income per person, averaged globally, rises by about 0.8 percent per year, but in more than one hundred countries, income has actually dropped since 1985. So has individual consumption in more than sixty countries. See James Gustave Speth's "The Plight of the Poor," *Foreign Affairs*, May–June 1999. See also Thomas Homer-Dixon's *The Ingenuity Gap* (Toronto and New York: Knopf, 2000).
4. Estimate by Manuel Castells, professor of sociology, University of California, Berkeley, and author of the trilogy *The Information Age: Economy, Society and Culture.*
5. See Burckhardt's *The Civilization of the Renaissance in Italy* (New York: Random House, 1954), p. 46.

6. See Fareed Zakaria's "The Rise of Illiberal Democracy," *Foreign Affairs,* Nov.–Dec. 1997.

7. Quoted in an Associated Press report by Memli Krasniqi, Jan. 1, 2000.

8. David K. Taylor, a demographer for the city of Tucson.

9. See James Salter's excellent "Once Upon a Time, Literature. Now What?" *The New York Times,* Sept. 13, 1999. Salter quotes novelist Don DeLillo about the masses inhabiting cities.

10. According to Joel E. Cohen, professor of populations at Rockefeller University, it is estimated that in 2006, 50 percent of humanity will live in urban conditions; by 2050, that number will rise to 85 percent.

11. See Winn Schwartau's "Asymmetrical Adversaries: Looming Security Threats," *Orbis,* Spring 2000.

12. Dr. Brian Sullivan, paper on space doctrine for U.S. Space Command.

13. The concepts "driving forces" and "sideswipes" were used in a lecture by Steven Bernow, of the Energy Group Tellus Institute of Boston, on Sept. 11, 2000, in New Paltz, New York.

14. See Carl E. Schorske's *Thinking with History: Explorations in the Passage to Modernism* (Princeton, N.J.: Princeton University Press, 1998), pp. 3–4.

15. See Raymond Aron's essays "Clausewitz" and "D'une sainte famille à l'autre," quoted in Tony Judt's *The Burden of Responsibility: Blum, Camus, Aron, and the French Twentieth Century* (Chicago: University of Chicago Press, 1998), p. 158.

16. See Barbara W. Tuchman's *Stilwell and the American Experience in China, 1911–45* (New York: Macmillan, 1970), p. 123.

17. From Marshall's address at Princeton University on Feb. 22, 1947.

CHAPTER II: CHURCHILL'S *RIVER WAR*

1. John Keegan, "His Finest Hour," *U.S. News & World Report,* May 29, 2000.

2. Isaiah Berlin, "Winston Churchill in 1940," in his *The Proper Study of Mankind: An Anthology of Essays* (New York: Farrar, Straus and

Giroux, 1998). The essay on Churchill first appeared in 1949, in *The Atlantic Monthly*.

3. Winston S. Churchill, *The River War: An Historical Account of the Re-Conquest of the Soudan*, 2 vols. (London: Longmans, Green, 1899; reprint, London: Prion, 1997, and South Bend, Ind.: St. Augustine Press, 2002).

4. Churchill, *The River War*, Prion, pp. 4–6, 63.

5. Ibid., pp. 122, 160, 161, 164, 182, 193.

6. Churchill, *The River War*, original, p. 14.

7. Churchill, *The River War*, Prion, p. 9.

8. See Arthur Hugh Clough's 1864 introduction to Plutarch's *The Lives of the Noble Grecians and Romans* (New York: Modern Library, 1992).

9. From Churchill's 1933 introduction to an edited version of *The River War*: Prion, p. xiii.

10. See Paul A. Rahe, "*The River War*: Nature's Provision, Man's Desire to Prevail, and the Prospects for Peace," in *Churchill as Peacemaker*, ed. James W. Muller (Cambridge, Eng.: Cambridge University Press, 1997). Also see *The River War*, original, pp. 18–19.

11. Churchill, *The River War*, Prion, p. 69.

12. Churchill, *The River War*, original, p. 35.

13. See Rahe's essay in *Churchill as Peacemaker*, pp. 82–119.

14. Churchill, *The River War*, original, pp. 19–20.

15. See Sallust, *The Jugurthine War*, trans. S. A. Handford (New York: Penguin, 1963), p. 77.

16. See C. Maurice Bowra's *The Greek Experience* (New York: World, 1957), chs. 2 and 10.

17. See Rahe.

CHAPTER III: LIVY'S PUNIC WAR

1. Jonathan Swift, *Gulliver's Travels* (New York: Knopf, 1991), p. 90.

2. Ibid., p. 55.

3. See Plutarch's *The Lives of the Noble Grecians and Romans*, vols. 1 and

2, trans. John Dryden, ed. Arthur Hugh Clough (New York: Modern Library, 1992). Although Plutarch lived at the beginning of the Christian era, he was a priest at the pagan temple of Delphi.

4. Ibid., vol. 1, p. 322.

5. See Seneca's *Moral and Political Essays,* ed. John M. Cooper and J. F. Procope (Cambridge, Eng.: Cambridge University Press, 1995), pp. 15, 155.

6. See Cicero's *Selected Works,* trans. and introduced by Michael Grant (New York: Penguin, 1960), p. 168.

7. Professor Donald Kagan writes: "Like the Hannibalic War, the Second World War emerged from flaws in the previous peace and the failure of the victors to alter or vigilantly and vigorously to defend the settlement they imposed." *On the Origins of War and the Preservation of Peace* (New York: Doubleday, 1995), p. 281.

8. See Livy's *The War with Hannibal,* trans. Aubrey de Sélincourt and introducted by Betty Radice (New York: Penguin, 1965), p. 182. All quotes from Livy unless otherwise noted are from the 1972 paperback edition.

9. Of the 142 books, all but thirty-five have been lost.

10. See the essay by Oxford professor and curator of the Bodleian Library Henry Francis Pelham, in the 11th edition of *The Encyclopaedia Britannica* (New York, 1910–11). Of the two, Virgil was more given to triumphalism than Horace, who occasionally shows a fine sense of the fragility of power.

11. See Andrew Feldherr's *Spectacle and Society in Livy's History* (Berkeley: University of California Press, 1998), p. 120. The Brutus and Scaevola episodes are in Livy's second book in his history of Rome.

12. In Book Three of Livy's history of Rome.

13. See Feldherr, p. 120.

14. See Betty Radice's introduction to the Penguin edition of *The War with Hannibal.*

15. Livy's *The War with Hannibal,* p. 23. Livy's words echo those of Thucydides in Book One of *The Peloponnesian War,* where he says he wrote his book because he foresaw that it would be history's greatest war.

16. See the section on Hitler in John Keegan's *The Mask of Command* (New York: Viking Penguin, 1987).

17. In fact, Rome's earlier entries into Corsica and Sardinia were also breaches of the treaty. Professor Donald Kagan, in his excellent book, writes that the peace Rome had imposed on Carthage "was of the least stable kind: it embittered the losers without depriving them of the capacity for seeking revenge. . . ." See *On the Origins of War*, p. 255.

18. Ibid., p. 273.

19. Livy's *The War with Hannibal*, p. 154.

20. Ibid., pp. 154–55.

21. See Susan Raven's *Rome in Africa* (London: Evans Brothers, 1969), ch. 3: "The Wars Between Rome and Carthage."

22. Ibid.

23. Ibid., p. 172.

24. See Betty Radice's introduction to the Penguin edition of *The War with Hannibal*.

25. Livy's *The War with Hannibal*, p. 120.

26. Ibid., p. 139.

27. Ibid., pp. 102–103.

28. Ibid., p. 42.

29. See Raymond Aron's *Peace and War: A Theory of International Relations*, trans. Richard Howard and Annette Baker Fox (Garden City, N.Y.: Doubleday, 1966), p. 305.

30. Ibid., pp. 96–100. Not only World War II and Vietnam, but Masada, too. The mass suicide of Jewish resistance fighters against Rome in 73 A.D. bears some resemblance to the mass suicide of the senators of Saguntum, in Spain, in 218 B.C., prior to their capture by Hannibal.

CHAPTER IV: SUN-TZU AND THUCYDIDES

1. See Karl von Clausewitz's *On War*, trans. O. L. Matthijs (New York: Random House, 1943), p. 299. All page references are to the 2000

Modern Library paperback edition, published in combination with Sun-Tzu's *The Art of Warfare*.

2. See Machiavelli's *Discourses on Livy*, trans. Julia Conaway Bondanella and Peter Bondanella (New York: Oxford University Press, 1997), p. 30, and Cicero's *Selected Works*, trans. and introduced by Michael Grant (New York: Penguin, 1960).

3. A poll of fifty-eight historians, conducted by C-SPAN and released on Feb. 21, 2000, ranked Reagan eleventh in overall performance of forty-one presidents. Jimmy Carter, who preceded him, ranked twenty-second, and George Bush, who succeeded him, twentieth. Richard Reeves, a noted historian and analyst, rated Reagan the most effective of recent presidents, though the least intellectual. See his survey in *George*, Feb. 2000.

4. Though Clausewitz ultimately rejected Kant's idealism, he nevertheless benefited from exposure to it.

5. See Machiavelli's *Discourses on Livy*, p. 351.

6. See Confucius's *The Analects*, trans. Raymond Dawson (New York: Oxford University Press, 1993), Book 7:1, p. 24.

7. See Ralph Peters's introduction to *The Art of Warfare* in the 2000 Modern Library paperback edition.

8. See Confucius's *Analects*, 12:20, p. 47.

9. See Plutarch's "Comparison of Romulus with Theseus," in vol. 1 of his *The Lives of the Noble Grecians and Romans*, trans. John Dryden, ed. Arthur Hugh Clough (New York: Modern Library, 1992), p. 50.

10. See Sun-Tzu's *The Art of Warfare*, pp. 123, 125.

11. Sima Qian, *Records of the Grand Historian: Han Dynasty I and II, Qin Dynasty*, trans. Burton Watson (New York: Columbia University Press, 1961), p. 187.

12. See José Ortega y Gasset's *Toward a Philosophy of History* (New York: Norton, 1941); retitled *History as a System* (New York: Norton, 1962), pp. 266–67.

13. See Anastasia Bakolas's unpublished Wellesley College monograph "Human Nature in Thucydides."

14. From a conversation with Robert B. Strassler, editor of *The Landmark Thucydides: A Comprehensive Guide to the Peloponnesian War* (New York: Free Press, 1996). Strassler's book, replete with maps, a footnoted translation of Thucydides' text, and time charts, is the best introduction to a complicated war. However, for a detailed exploration of the Peace of Nicias, as it is properly called, see Donald Kagan's *The Peace of Nicias and the Sicilian Expedition* (Ithaca, N.Y.: Cornell University Press, 1981).

15. See Thucydides' *The Peloponnesian War,* trans. Thomas Hobbes (Chicago: University of Chicago Press, 1989); W. Robert Connor's *Thucydides* (Princeton, N.J.: Princeton University Press, 1984); and Bakolas's "Human Nature in Thucydides."

16. Ibid.

17. See Thucydides' *The Peloponnesian War,* V:89, p. 365 for Hobbes's more beautiful but harder to follow translation: "Both you and we knowing that in human disputation justice is only agreed on when the necessity is equal; whereas they that have odds of power exact as much as they can, and the weak yield to such conditions as they can get." Here, I have used the 1874 translation by Richard Crawley in *The Landmark Thucydides,* p. 352.

18. See *The Peloponnesian War,* IV:65; *The Landmark Thucydides,* p. 258.

19. See Peter Green's *Classical Bearings: Interpreting Ancient History and Culture* (Berkeley: University of California Press, 1989), p. 24.

20. See "The Reinvention of Hatred" in Geoffrey Hartman's *A Critic's Journey* (New Haven, Conn.: Yale University Press, 1999).

21. For an example of how conflict brings out the worst in human beings, see *The Peloponnesian War,* III:82; *The Landmark Thucydides,* pp. 199–200.

22. See Aron's *Peace and War: A Theory of International Relations,* trans. Richard Howard and Annette Baker Fox (Garden City, N.Y.: Doubleday, 1966), p. 321; Ortega y Gasset's *The Revolt of the Masses,* trans. Anthony Kerrigan (South Bend, Ind.: University of Notre Dame Press, 1985), p. 129; and Clausewitz's *On War,* p. 357.

23. See Ian McGreal's summary of Sun-Tzu in *Great Literature of the Eastern World* (New York: HarperCollins, 1996).

24. Aron, *Peace and War,* p. 300.

25. Ibid., p. 307.

26. See Gress's *From Plato to NATO: The Idea of the West and Its Opponents* (New York: Free Press, 1998), p. 1.

CHAPTER V: MACHIAVELLIAN VIRTUE

1. See Professor Lawrence F. Hundersmarck's essay on Machiavelli in *Great Thinkers of the Western World,* ed. Ian P. McGreal (New York: HarperCollins, 1992). Machiavelli's criticism of Christianity is related to that of Friedrich Nietzsche, who believed that by equating meekness with goodness, Christianity justified, albeit indirectly, inaction and mediocrity.

2. See Harvey C. Mansfield's *Machiavelli's Virtue* (Chicago: University of Chicago Press, 1996), pp. 20, 33.

3. See Aron's article in *Esprit,* quoted in Tony Judt's *The Burden of Responsibility: Blum, Camus, Aron, and the French Twentieth Century* (Chicago: University of Chicago Press, 1998), p. 150.

4. See the account of Patrick Tyler, *The New York Times* Beijing bureau chief, in *A Great Wall: Six Presidents and China; an Investigative History* (New York: The Century Foundation/Public Affairs, 1999).

5. See "What Is the Timor Message?" *The Wall Street Journal,* Sept. 29, 1999.

6. See Berlin's essay "The Originality of Machiavelli," in his collection *The Proper Study of Mankind* (New York: Farrar, Straus and Giroux, 1998). Montesquieu, too, made the distinction between "*political* virtue" and "Christian virtue"; see his *The Spirit of the Laws,* trans. Anne M. Cohler, Basia Carolyn Miller, and Harold Samuel Stone (New York: Cambridge University Press, 1989), p. xli.

7. For a long discussion of Sallust's concept of public virtue, see D. C.

Earl's *The Political Thought of Sallust* (Cambridge, Eng.: Cambridge University Press, 1961).

8. See Russell Price's appendix in his translation of *The Prince*, listed under Machiavelli in the bibliography. See also Plutarch, *The Lives of the Noble Grecians and Romans*, vol. 1, trans. John Dryden, ed. Arthur Hugh Clough (New York: Modern Library, 1992), p. 291.

9. See Miller's essay "American Playhouse," *Harper's*, June 2001.

10. See Mansfield's *Machiavelli's Virtue*, p. 61.

11. See Sun-Tzu's *The Art of Warfare*, trans. Roger T. Ames (New York: Ballantine, 1993), p. 74.

12. See William Manchester's *A World Lit Only by Fire: The Medieval Mind and the Renaissance*. First paperback edition, p. 100.

13. Quoted from Jacques Barzun's *From Dawn to Decadence: 500 Years of Western Cultural Life; 1500 to the Present* (New York: HarperCollins, 2000), p. 256. See also Machiavelli's *Florentine Histories*, trans. Harvey C. Mansfield and Laura Banfield (Princeton, N.J.: Princeton University Press, 1991).

14. Barzun, p. 256.

15. Ibid., p. 258.

16. Machiavelli was "*the* man of the Renaissance," writes Professor Harvey C. Mansfield. See Mansfield's *Machiavelli's Virtue*, p. 9.

17. See Thomas C. Schelling, *Arms and Influence* (New Haven, Conn.: Yale University Press, 1966).

18. See Lincoln's second annual message to Congress, December 1962.

19. See Mark Grimsley's *The Hard Hand of War: Union Military Policy Toward Southern Civilians, 1861–1865* (New York: Cambridge University Press, 1995).

20. The Fraser Institute, "Economic Freedom of the World," *The Economist*, Sept. 11, 1999.

21. *Federalist No. 6.*

22. *Federalist No. 14.* See also *Federalist No. 10.*

23. See Mansfield's *Machiavelli's Virtue*, p. 88.

24. Ibid. Machiavelli's idea is not completely new. Thucydides, for example, praises Pericles for his "foresight" (*pronoia*).

CHAPTER VI: FATE AND INTERVENTION

1. See Polybius's *The Rise of the Roman Empire*, trans. Ian Scott-Kilvert (New York: Penguin, 1979), pp. 183–84.
2. The postcolonial decades saw the Algerian population double about every generation, while the number of urban dwellers relative to the rest of the population often grew by more than 5 percent annually. Sources include the Population Reference Bureau and the World Bank.
3. See the various Human Development Indexes published annually by the United Nations Development Programme.
4. See Berlin's essay by that name in his *Four Essays on Liberty* (Oxford, Eng.: Oxford University Press, 1969).
5. See Norman Stone's "There Is No Such Thing as Inevitability," *The Sunday Telegraph*, Feb. 28, 1999.
6. Sima Qian, *Records of the Grand Historian: Han Dynasty I and II, Qin Dynasty*, trans. Burton Watson (New York: Columbia University Press, 1961), pp. 12–13.
7. See Toynbee's *A Study of History* (Oxford, Eng.: Oxford University Press, 1946), p. 247.
8. See Isaiah Berlin's essay " 'From Hope and Fear Set Free' " in his *The Proper Study of Mankind* (New York: Farrar, Straus and Giroux, 1998).
9. See Albert Wohlstetter, "Bishops, Statesmen, and Other Strategists on the Bombing of Innocents," *Commentary*, June 1983; and the letters in response (by Bruce Russett, Samuel Huntington, and Brent Scowcroft) and Wohlstetter's reply in the Dec. 1983 issue.
10. See Michael Howard's review of John Lukacs's *Five Days in London, May 1940* in *The National Interest*, Spring 2000.

11. See Edmund Morris's *Dutch: A Memoir of Ronald Reagan* (New York: Random House, 1999), p. 413.

12. See Michael Ignatieff's *Isaiah Berlin: A Life* (New York: Holt, 1998), in particular p. 24.

13. The essay is included in Berlin's *Four Essays on Liberty*.

14. See Ignatieff's *Isaiah Berlin*, p. 200.

15. See Berlin's "The Counter-Enlightenment" in *The Proper Study of Mankind*.

16. See Berlin's introduction to *Four Essays on Liberty*.

17. See Valerie Percival and Thomas Homer-Dixon, "Environmental Scarcity and Violent Conflict: The Case of Rwanda," monograph, University of Toronto, 1995; "World Population Data Sheet, 1992," Population Reference Bureau, Washington, D.C.; and Stanley Meisler, "Rwanda and Burundi," *The Atlantic Monthly*, Sept. 1973.

18. See Daniel J. Mahoney's excellent article "Three Decent Frenchmen," a review of Tony Judt's *The Burden of Responsibility*, which appeared in *The National Interest*, Summer 1999. See also *History, Truth and Liberty: Selected Writings of Raymond Aron*, ed. Franciszek Draus (Chicago: University of Chicago Press, 1985).

19. See Barbara Tuchman's *Stilwell and the American Experience in China, 1911–45* (New York: Macmillan, 1970), p. 178. See, too, "Ghosts from China and Japan," *The Economist*, Jan. 29, 2000. Some casualty estimates for Nanking are as high as 300,000.

20. See Book I of Machiavelli's *Discourses on Livy*, trans. Julia Conaway Bondanella and Peter Bondanella (New York: Oxford University Press, 1997), and Mansfield's *Machiavelli's Virtue* (Chicago: University of Chicago Press, 1996), p. 75.

21. See Mansfield, p. 116.

22. See Ralph Peters's *Fighting for the Future: Will America Triumph?* (Mechanicsburg, Pa.: Stackpole, 1999) and Joseph Conrad's *Heart of Darkness* (1902).

CHAPTER VII: THE GREAT DISTURBERS:
HOBBES AND MALTHUS

1. See Leo Strauss, *The Political Philosophy of Hobbes: Its Basis and Its Genesis,* trans. Elsa M. Sinclair (Oxford, Eng.: Clarendon, 1936), p. 49.

2. Unless indicated otherwise, my summary of Hobbes's philosophy comes—in addition from Hobbes himself—from the 1966 University of Chicago Press edition of Strauss's book. Strauss's writing about Hobbes and other philosophers has often shown more clarity than that of later generations of academics, who have often been critical of Strauss. But even Strauss's critics admit that his book on Hobbes was his best.

3. *Federalist No. 15* and *Federalist No. 51.*

4. *Federalist No. 70.*

5. From Hobbes's *De Homine* (1658). See Strauss, p. 9.

6. Strauss, pp. 17, 22.

7. See Job 41:34 and Hobbes, *Leviathan,* ch. 28.

8. See *The Politics of Aristotle,* trans. Peter L. Phillips Simpson (Chapel Hill: University of North Carolina Press, 1997). For instance, Book 1, chs. 1 and 2, pp. 8, 12.

9. Ibn Khaldu'n, *The Muqaddimah: An Introduction to History,* trans. Franz Rosenthal (Princeton, N.J.: Bollingen/Princeton University Press, 1958), ch. 1: First Prefatory Discussion, p. 47.

10. Strauss, pp. 60–61, and *Leviathan,* ch. 17.

11. Ibid.

12. *Leviathan,* ch. 15.

13. Ibid.

14. See Christina Lamb and Philip Sherwell's "Sandline Boss Blames Blair for Carnage in Sierra Leone," *The Sunday Telegraph,* May 14, 2000.

15. From Berlin's *Four Essays on Liberty,* quoted by John Gray in *Berlin* (New York: Fontana/HarperCollins, 1995), p. 141. Berlin wrote this in

the context of explaining the ideas of the nineteenth-century Russian liberal intellectual Alexander Herzen.

16. See Huntington's *Political Order in Changing Societies* (New Haven, Conn.: Yale University Press, 1968), p. 1.

17. Strauss, pp. 25–26.

18. The italics are Madison's. See *Federalist No. 10.*

19. *Federalist No. 17* and *Federalist No. 38.* Solon confessed to giving his people not the government best suited to their happiness, "but most tolerable to their prejudices."

20. *Federalist No. 85.*

21. See Francis Fukuyama's *The End of History and the Last Man* (New York: Free Press, 1992), p. 154. See also Thomas L. Pangle and Peter J. Ahrensdorf, *Justice Among Nations: On the Moral Basis of Power and Peace* (Lawrence: University Press of Kansas, 1999), p. 150. Aristotle writes that the best regimes are those "that look to the common advantage"; see Simpson's *The Politics of Aristotle,* p. 88.

22. See Huntington's *Political Order in Changing Societies,* p. 102.

23. Professor Burton M. Leiser writes that "Hobbes anticipated many of the major principles that went into the founding of the American republic"; see Leiser's essay on Hobbes in Ian P. McGreal, *Great Thinkers of the Western World* (New York: HarperCollins, 1992).

24. *Federalist No. 51.*

25. Ibid.

26. Ibid.

27. *Federalist No. 49.*

28. See Harvey C. Mansfield's *Machiavelli's Virtue* (Chicago: University of Chicago Press, 1996), pp. 293–94. See also the commentary by Carnes Lord in Machiavelli's *The Prince,* ed. and trans. Angelo M. Codevilla (New Haven, Conn.: Yale University Press, 1997).

29. Mansfield, pp. 293–94. See Hamilton's *Federalist No. 6* on deceitful utopias and Paul A. Rahe's *Republics Ancient and Modern* (Chapel Hill: University of North Carolina Press, 1994).

30. See Rahe's *Republics Ancient and Modern,* vol. 2: *New Modes & Orders in Early Modern Political Thought,* pp. 94–95.

31. In *Republics Ancient and Modern,* vol. 3: *Inventions of Prudence: Constituting the American Regime,* p. 172, Rahe writes: "Madison and his colleagues . . . never seriously doubted that the United States of America was—like ancient Sparta, though in a radically different fashion— a mixed regime. . . ." See, too, Michael A. Ledeen's *Machiavelli on Modern Leadership: Why Machiavelli's Iron Rules Are as Timely and Important Today as Five Centuries Ago* (New York: St. Martin's, 1999), p. 109.

32. See Michael Oakeshott's "Introduction to *Leviathan*" in Hobbes's *Leviathan,* ed. Richard E. Flathman and David Johnston (New York: Norton, 1997).

33. William Godwin, *An Inquiry Concerning Political Justice and Its Influence on General Virtue and Happiness,* 1793. Marquis de Condorcet, *Sketch for a Historical Picture of the Progress of the Human Mind,* 1795.

34. See Cornell University scholar David Price's "Of Population and False Hopes: Malthus and His Legacy," *Population and Environment: A Journal of Interdisciplinary Studies,* Jan. 1998. See also Malthus's *An Essay on the Principle of Population,* ed. Philip Appleman (New York: Norton, 1988), pp. 122, 110.

35. See Nora Barlow's *The Autobiography of Charles Darwin* (London: Collins, 1958). See also John F. Rohe's *A Bicentennial Malthusian Essay* (Traverse City, Mich.: Rhodes & Easton, 1997).

36. See Professor Philip Appleman's introduction to Malthus's *Essay,* under Malthus in the bibliography.

37. See Ronald Bailey's "The Law of Increasing Returns," *The National Interest,* Spring 2000.

38. See Appleman's essay.

39. See F. L. Jones, *The Letters of Percy Bysshe Shelley* (New York: Oxford University Press, 1964). Shelley's similarly radical and self-righteous attacks on the pragmatic and successful statesmanship of Viscount Castlereagh may have contributed to the latter's suicide in 1822.

40. Charles Dickens, *A Christmas Carol* (London, 1843). See, too, Appleman's introduction to Malthus's *Essay* and Rohe's *Bicentennial Essay*.

41. See L. Meek's *Marx and Engels on the Population Bomb* (Berkeley: University of California Press, 1971).

42. See Mill's 1864 book *Principles of Political Economy with Some of Their Applications to Social Philosophy*.

43. See Malthus's *Essay on the Principle of Population*, p. 124.

44. See Jack A. Goldstone's *Revolution and Rebellion in the Early Modern World* (Berkeley: University of California Press, 1991).

45. See Mayra Buvinic and Andrew R. Morrison's excellent article "Living in a More Violent World," *Foreign Policy,* Spring 2000. Global homicide rates jumped by 50 percent in the 1990s: 15 percent in the industrialized world, 80 percent in Latin America, and 112 percent in the Arab world, for example.

46. See Robert Evans, "Report Warns of Impact of Global Warming," Reuters, Feb. 19, 2001.

47. See Vaclav Smil's *China's Environmental Crisis: An Inquiry into the Limits of National Development* (Armonk, N.Y.: Sharpe, 1993).

CHAPTER VIII: THE HOLOCAUST, REALISM, AND KANT

1. See Novick's *The Holocaust in American Life* (Boston: Houghton Mifflin, 1999), pp. 91–98. See also Eva Hoffman's "The Uses of Hell," *The New York Review of Books,* March 9, 2000.

2. See Hilene Flanzbaum's *The Americanization of the Holocaust* (Baltimore, Md.: Johns Hopkins University Press, 1999), pp. 10–11.

3. Ibid., p. 11. Also, Novick (p. 128) writes that Shirer devotes only 2 or 3 percent of his 1,200-page book to the murder of European Jewry; thus the influence of his book on the growth of Holocaust awareness should not be overstated.

4. Novick, p. 190.

5. For a concise description of different levels of altruism drawn partly

from other sources, see Chapter 6 of Carl Coon's *Culture Wars and the Global Village* (Amherst, N.Y.: Prometheus, 2000).

6. See Anatol Lieven's *"Qu'est-ce qu'une nation?"* in *The National Interest,* Fall 1997.

7. See Michael Ignatieff's *Isaiah Berlin* (New York: Holt, 1998), p. 245; Raymond Aron's *Peace and War: A Theory of International Relations* (Garden City, N.Y.: Doubleday, 1966), pp. 149, 163; and *The Federalist Papers,* under Alexander Hamilton in the bibliography, pp. 110–11, 233, 308, 314–15, 322, 360–61.

8. See Marguerite Yourcenar's *Memoirs of Hadrian* (New York: Farrar, Straus and Giroux, 1990), p. 116. Though a fictional memoir, it was meticulously researched and likely gives as accurate a picture of Hadrian's thoughts as any historian could manage.

9. See Michael Grant's translation of Cicero's *Selected Works* (New York: Penguin, 1971), p. 168.

10. See Henry Kissinger's *Diplomacy* (New York: Simon & Schuster, 1994); also Carsten Holbraad's *The Concert of Europe: A Study in German and British International Theory, 1815–1914* (London: Longmans, 1970); and A. N. Wilson's *Eminent Victorians* (New York: Norton, 1989).

11. Henry L. Stimson and McGeorge Bundy, *On Active Service in Peace and War* (New York: Harper & Brothers, 1948), p. 259.

12. See Kissinger, p. 372.

13. See Robert Dallek's *Franklin D. Roosevelt and American Foreign Policy, 1932–1945* (New York: Oxford University Press, 1979), p. 520.

14. Ibid.

15. See Adams's *Works* (Boston: Little, Brown, 1850–56), 4:401.

16. *Federalist No. 8.*

17. See Otto Hintze's "Calvinism and *Raison d'état*" in *The Historical Essays of Otto Hintze,* edited with an introduction by Felix Gilbert (New York: Oxford University Press, 1975).

18. See Kennan's *Realities of American Foreign Policy* (Princeton, N.J.: Princeton University Press, 1954).

19. See Arthur Schlesinger Jr.'s *The Cycles of American History* (Boston: Houghton Mifflin, 1986); quoted in George Kennan's *At a Century's Ending: Reflections, 1982–1995* (New York: Norton, 1996), p. 213. Kennan notes that Schlesinger's viewpoint is "firmly rooted in Federalist thinking. . . ."

20. See Barbara Tuchman's *Stilwell and the American Experience in China, 1911–45* (New York: Macmillan, 1970), p. 134.

21. See Fareed Zakaria's "Is Realism Finished?" *The National Interest,* Winter 1992–93.

22. Ibid.

23. *Chan-kuo Ts'e,* trans. J. I. Crump (Ann Arbor: University of Michigan Press, 1973), pp. 124–25.

24. In *Federalist No. 6,* Hamilton shows how commercial republics from Athens to eighteenth-century Britain have frequently been engaged in war. While "the people compose one branch of the national legislature" in Britain, few nations "have been more frequently engaged in war": wars which "in numerous instances, proceeded from the people."

25. See C. M. Bowra's *The Greek Experience* (New York: Mentor, 1957), p. 88.

26. Ibid.

27. *Federalist No. 6.*

28. See Barzun's *From Dawn to Decadence: 500 Years of Western Cultural Life; 1500 to the Present* (New York: HarperCollins, 2000), p. 52.

29. See Lothar Gall's *Bismarck: The White Revolutionary,* vol. 1, *1851–1871* (London: Unwin Hyman,), pp. 29, 92.

30. See Wills's *Saint Augustine* (New York: Lipper/Viking, 1999), p. 119. See also Thomas L. Pangle and Peter J. Ahrendorf's *Justice Among Nations: On the Moral Basis of Power and Peace* (Lawrence: University Press of Kansas, 1999), p. 75. In Augustine's *City of God,* see in particular Books 15 and 19.

31. Immanuel Kant, *Groundwork of the Metaphysics of Morals,* trans. Mary Gregor and introduced by Christine M. Korsgaard (New York: Cam-

bridge University Press, 1997). All page notations are from this edition, in the series Cambridge Texts in the History of Philosophy.

32. See Kant's essay "To Perpetual Peace: A Philosophical Sketch," 1795.

33. Kant, *Groundwork of the Metaphysics of Morals,* p. 19.

34. Ibid.

35. See Zakaria. See, too, Appendix 1 of Kant's essay "To Perpetual Peace."

36. Kant, *Groundwork of the Metaphysics of Morals,* p. 24. See, too, Christine Korsgaard's introduction.

37. Ibid., p. 31.

38. See Korsgaard's introduction to Kant.

39. Kant, *Groundwork of the Metaphysics of Morals,* p. 37.

40. See Professor J.J.C. Smart's defense of consequential morality in his and Bernard Williams's *Utilitarianism: For and Against* (Cambridge, Eng.: Cambridge University Press, 1973), p. 93.

41. See D. H. Hodgson's *Consequences of Utilitarianism* (London: Oxford University Press, 1967).

42. Cicero, "On Duties: III," *Selected Works,* p. 191.

43. See Harvey C. Mansfield's *Machiavelli's Virtue* (Chicago: University of Chicago Press, 1996), p. 8.

CHAPTER IX: THE WORLD OF ACHILLES:
ANCIENT SOLDIERS, MODERN WARRIORS

1. See Seneca's "On Anger" in his *Moral and Political Essays,* ed. John M. Cooper and J. F. Procope (Cambridge, Eng.: Cambridge University Press, 1995), pp. 41, 28.

2. See Dana Priest's "A Four-Star Foreign Policy?" *The Washington Post,* Sept. 28, 2000. See also my essay "The Dangers of Peace" in *The Coming Anarchy* (New York: Random House, 2000).

3. For the statistics on moving brigades and divisions, see Stephen P. Aubin's "Stumbling Toward Transformation: How the Services Stack Up," *Strategic Review,* Spring 2000.

4. See Raymond Aron's *Peace and War: A Theory of International Relations*, trans. Richard Howard and Annette Baker Fox (Garden City, N.Y.: Doubleday, 1966), p. 305.

5. See Ralph Peters's *Fighting for the Future: Will America Triumph?* (Mechanicsburg, Pa.: Stackpole, 1999), p. 32.

6. See *The Iliad*, trans. Robert Fagles (New York: Penguin, 1990), Book 19, line 179.

7. Ibid., lines 254–65.

8. See James Der Derian's "Battlefield of Tomorrow: Netwar," *Wired*, July 7, 1999.

9. See Knox's introduction to the Fagles translation of *The Iliad*.

10. See Knox's introduction, as well as Weil's "*The Iliad;* or, The Poem of Force," translated by Mary McCarthy and not published until 1945 in *Politics* magazine.

11. *The Iliad*, Fagles translation, Book 8, lines 638–42.

12. See Peters, pp. 109–10.

13. This is a point made in the separate writings of two Washington analysts, Reuel Marc Gerecht and Edward Luttwak.

14. For a discussion on the legality of assassination, see Mark Vincent Vlasic's "Cloak and Dagger Diplomacy: The U.S. and Assassination" in the *Georgetown Journal of International Affairs*, Summer/Fall 2000.

15. See Luttwak's prescient article "Toward Post-Heroic Warfare," *Foreign Affairs*, May–June 1995.

16. See Ignatieff's *Virtual War: Kosovo and Beyond* (New York: Holt, 2000), p. 179.

17. See Cronkite's interview with *Playboy*, June 1973, p. 76.

18. Ibid., pp. 184, 213–14.

19. See Sun-Tzu, *The Art of Warfare*, trans. Roger T. Ames (New York: Modern Library, 2000), pp. 80, 131.

20. Thucydides, *The Peloponnesian War*, Crawley translation, VI:23.

21. See Van Riper's "Information Superiority," *Marine Corps Gazette*, June 1997.

22. See Dunlap's "21st Century Land Warfare: Four Dangerous Myths," *Parameters,* U.S. Army War College, Carlisle, Pennsylvania, Autumn 1997.

23. Michael Lind, "The Honor Paradigm and International Ethics," unpublished.

24. See Kenneth Waltz's *Theory of International Politics* (New York: McGraw-Hill, 1979).

25. See Knox's *Backing into the Future: The Classical Tradition and Its Renewal* (New York: Norton, 1994), pp. 11–12.

CHAPTER X: WARRING STATES
CHINA AND GLOBAL GOVERNANCE

1. From a conversation with Robert Strassler, author of *The Landmark Thucydides: A Comprehensive Guide to the Peloponnesian War* (New York: Free Press, 1996).

2. See Strassler's Epilogue to *The Landmark Thucydides.*

3. See my article "Could This Be the New World?" *The New York Times,* Dec. 27, 1999.

4. According to the Population Reference Bureau, India's population will rise from 1 billion to 1.6 billion during the first half of the twenty-first century, while Africa's will rise from 800 million to 1.8 billion by 2050, even after subtracting AIDS-related deaths.

5. See Adam Watson's *The Evolution of International Society: A Comparative Analysis* (New York: Routledge, 1992). Much of the material in the paragraphs that follow is inspired by this brilliant book.

6. See Watson, p. 81, paperback.

7. Watson, Chapter 8, various encyclopedias, translations of Hsun-tzu, etc.

8. Watson, p. 121.

9. See Montesquieu's *The Spirit of the Laws,* trans. Anne M. Cohler, Basia Carolyn Miller, and Harold Samuel Stone (New York: Cambridge Uni-

versity Press, 1989), in particular, Book 1, Chapter 3, p. 7 and Book 10, Chapter 3, p. 139. See, too, Thomas L. Pangle and Peter J. Ahrensdorf, *Justice Among Nations* (Lawrence: University Press of Kansas, 1999), p. 157.

10. See Carr's *The Twenty Years' Crisis, 1919–1939* (New York: Harper & Row, 1946), p. 107. Carr, of course, was also a pro-Soviet historian. But that does not detract from some fine points he makes in *The Twenty Years' Crisis,* which is not about the Soviet Union.

11. See Carr, p. 232.

12. See Jessica Mathews's "Power Shift," *Foreign Affairs,* Jan.–Feb. 1997.

13. Letter to John Quinn, May 6, 1917, New York Public Library. Quoted in Z. Najder's *Joseph Conrad: A Chronicle* (Cambridge, Eng.: Cambridge University Press, 1983), p. 424.

14. See Sun-Tzu's *The Art of Warfare* (New York: Modern Library, 2000), p. 91.

15. See George Cawkwell's introduction to Xenophon's *The Persian Expedition* (New York: Penguin, 1972). Xenophon's army was retreating back to Greece after an ill-fated attempt to help Cyrus the Younger secure the throne of Persia.

16. See Brzezinski's *The Grand Chessboard: American Primacy and Its Geostrategic Imperatives* (New York: Basic Books, 1997), p. 36.

CHAPTER XI: TIBERIUS

1. See the 11th edition of *The Encyclopaedia Britannica* (New York, 1910–11).

2. Ibid. There is also the accident of Tiberius's emperorship at the time Jesus was slain in a far-off Roman province.

3. See Levick's *Tiberius: The Politician* (London: Routledge, 1999), p. 85.

4. Ibid., pp. 138–39, 142–45. The city of Tiberias on the Sea of Galilee was, in fact, built by Herod Antipas.

5. Ibid., p. 178. Levick draws upon Tacitus's *Annales,* VI, 48, 4.

6. See especially Montesquieu's *Considerations on the Causes of the Greatness of the Romans and Their Decline,* trans. David Lowenthal (Indianapolis: Hackett, 1999).

7. Tacitus praises Tiberius for this action. See Tacitus, *Annales,* IV, 72, and Levick, pp. 136, 223.

8. See the 11th edition of *The Encyclopaedia Britannica.*

9. See D. H. Lawrence's *Studies in Classic American Literature* (New York: Viking, 1923 and 1971), p. 111.

INDEX